I am the Lord that

HEALETH

thee

I am the Lord that
HEALETH
thee

DICK IVERSON
&
WENDELL SMITH

The City™
CHURCH

I AM THE LORD THAT HEALETH THEE
Dick Iverson & Wendell Smith

A publication of The City Church
9051 132nd Ave NE Kirkland, WA 98033. USA
425-803-3233
www.thecity.org

Cover Design by Sean Sperte
Healing Icon by Andrew Chiu
Design & Layout by Katie Venti

All Scriptures are taken from the King James Version,
unless otherwise noted.

Contents

Dedication by Rev. Dick Iverson

To my beloved and faithful wife, Edie, who stood by me when God called us to foreign lands. She has stood by my side in spirit and in faith as we have ministered to thousands for nearly sixty years of ministry.

To the sick, diseased, afflicted, deaf, mute and blind. Our desire for you is that this book will bring to light the full Gospel of Jesus Christ and shine upon you to bring to pass a mighty deliverance in your life.

Foreword

Dick Iverson has been my Pastor since 1972. He is my spiritual father and mentor and has imparted many dynamic and wonderful things into my life and that of my family.

There are so many invaluable lessons and things I have learned from my Pastor over the years. It is always difficult to single out any particular truth or principle that someone has taught you. But more than any single thing I believe I received from our spiritual parents is the understanding of the vital importance of faith in every aspect of life as a believer.

Pastor Iverson began his ministry in the 1950s when he traveled first with Dr. T. L. Osborn and later on his own to the British Isles and ministered to thousands with a powerful word of faith and healing. Countless people who suffered from terrible physical afflictions were helped, healed and delivered through the faithful ministry of healing that was a hallmark of Dick Iverson's early ministry.

I was privileged to sit under his faith-filled pastoral ministry and serve on his staff for twenty years at Bible Temple (now City Bible Church) in Portland, Oregon. Little did I know that years later, having been sent out from his church to start our own, I would face the greatest challenge of my own life and faith and desperately need to access these truths of divine healing for myself. Diagnosed with a life-threatening cancer in 2004, the revelation of divine healing and its availability for us today, as taught in this book, would be the single most important key to bring healing and health to my own body and preserve my life.

Our church in Seattle, with thousands of members, is still being impacted weekly by the truths and revelations that were preached by Pastor Iverson over fifty years ago. Our people today are experiencing divine healing and finding health for their bodies because of the legacy we inherited from my Pastor.

I am eternally grateful for the faithful teaching of Brother Dick and his understanding of healing and the power of faith. It has saved my life. I believe, as you read, it could save yours as well.

Dr. Wendell E. Smith
Senior Pastor
The City Church of Seattle

I am the Lord that

HEALETH

thee

CHAPTER I

Where is Your Faith?

But He said to them, "Where is your faith?" And they were afraid, and marveled, saying to one another, "Who can this be? For He commands even the winds and water, and they obey Him!"

– Luke 8:25

The Confusion of "Faith"

When we first started our healing meetings in Northern Ireland in 1954, we had hundreds of people gather to hear the Word of God and to seek healing. We went from town to town and held two weeks of meetings in each area. Eventually, as the word spread about what was happening, those crowds grew until we were renting the largest auditoriums available in the country, seating more than five thousand people at one time. Each time it was predictable what would occur. People would come at first out of curiosity or in some cases desperation. But after one or two nights, and the preaching of the Word of God, lights would begin to go on in people's hearts and I could see that faith was being stirred in their hearts. My mentor and pastor, T.L. Osborn had taught us that faith comes by hearing and if we would simply teach the Word, eventually people would have the faith to believe for the supernatural.

There have been countless sermons on the great subject of faith. Theologians have told us what it will do and have explained the power that is available through faith. Many preachers and evangelists have declared how faith will drive out the enemy and move the hand of God to fulfill His promises. Yet so little is said concerning how we are to obtain faith and how we are to use it.

For years this powerful weapon of faith has been lying dormant in many of our lives and in many of our churches because of a lack of knowledge of how to put faith into action. We expect only the preacher or the evangelist to have faith. But this is wrong because God is not a "respecter of persons." The Bible says *"without faith it is impossible to please God"* (Hebrews 11:6). Can you imagine God telling His children that they cannot please Him unless they have this mystical thing called faith; and then telling them that He was going to keep faith a secret and make it hard for them to experience it? This would be foolish thinking. God says much in His Word concerning this all important subject called faith.

The Legal Side of Faith

Hebrews 11:1 and 6 says, *"Now faith is the substance of things hoped for, the evidence of things not seen;" "And without faith it is impossible to please Him: for he that cometh to God must believe that He is, and that He is a rewarder of them that diligently seek Him* (another translation says *"seriously seek Him"*). One writer declares that faith is the title deed of things not seen. The man who has a title deed to a home is legally the owner of that house, even though for some reason he may not have even seen it.

If you possess the title to a car you are the owner of that car, even though you have never driven it. Faith is the substance or title deed that declares you are the legal owner of the things you do not see. Faith in the promises of God is more real in the sight of God than even the natural evidence of the possession of the promises. Your faith in the promises makes them legally yours and no one can take them away from you. Just because you possess a car, you are not necessarily the legal owner of it. It takes the title deed to make you the legal owner of the automobile, not just the possession of it. God wants you to both believe and possess His glorious promises.

Hope is not Faith

Faith must have a reason. Why do you believe? You must have a reason for believing. Why do you believe God will save your soul? Why do you believe God will heal your body? Why do you believe God will supply your needs? Many of us just say, "I believe" without any reason for believing. Then we wonder why we fall or cannot maintain our healing or our assurance of salvation.

I have asked hundreds of people why they believe God will heal them and I have received scores of different answers, such as, "Oh, I just have faith" or "I know a friend who was healed so I believe I can be healed." "I have been a Christian for forty years, so I know God will heal me because I am so faithful and good."

Some have based their faith on what happened twenty years ago. Because they were healed twenty years ago they believe God should heal them again now. Many come into the prayer line just to try something out or because they are strong in hope. But to have producing faith you must have a reason for believing that God will do this or do that.

If a man said to me, "I have faith that I am going to meet you tomorrow at 10:00 p.m. in front of the post office," I would ask him, "How do you know I'll be there?" If he would answer me, "Oh, I just have faith you will be there," I would respond to this man, "Did I say I would be there?" He would answer me, "Oh, no, but I just have faith that you will be there." This man could not have faith that I would be there because I did not say I would. He only had hope although he called it faith.

Why do you believe God will heal you? Because God said so! *"Who forgiveth all thine iniquities, who healeth all thy diseases"* (Psalm 103:3). *"I am the Lord that healeth thee"* (Exodus 15:26). *"By His stripes ye were healed"* (1 Peter 2:24). Now you have grounds for faith—real, active, power-producing faith!

The Bible says, *"Faith cometh by hearing, and hearing by the Word of God"* (Romans 10:17). There is only one way you can have true faith and that is by hearing God's promises which covers the specific need in your life. The promise is the title deed declaring that you are legal owner of your deliverance. Faith is believing God's promises and acting accordingly.

I have heard so many people say that they "can't believe." Maybe you have used the very same words, "I just can't believe—I have no faith." Let me ask you this question, "Believe who? Who can you not believe?" I never have had a person yet tell me that they cannot believe God, and yet when we say, "I can't believe," we are telling God that we do not believe Him.

> *"God is not a man that He can lie; neither the son of man that He should repent: Hath He said, and shall He not do it? Or hath He spoken, and shall He not make it good?"*
>
> —Numbers 23:19

The Key to God's Promises

Romans 10:17, *"So then faith cometh by hearing, and hearing by the Word of God."* In this Scripture God tells us exactly how we can have faith. Many Christians have read this portion of Scripture and yet have never understood how simple it is to obtain faith that will move the hand of God. There are many Christians, including this author, who have prayed and fasted to obtain faith, but never obtained it. All the time faith had been before our eyes and even in our hands, as we handled the Word of God. Faith simply comes by hearing a promise of God which covers your need. The moment you believe, begin to act on the promise. That is faith! And our faith is in Jehovah –Rapha, the Lord our Healer!

> *"And said, If thou wilt diligently hearken to the voice of the LORD thy God, and wilt do that which is right in his sight, and wilt give ear to his commandments, and keep all his statutes, I will put none of these diseases upon thee, which I have brought upon the Egyptians:* **for I am the LORD that healeth thee (Jehovah Rapha)."**
>
> —Exodus 15:26

4

If you are sick you will rise up out of your sick bed acting on the promise, *"By His stripes ye were healed"* (1 Peter 2:24). You can embrace the promise that *"Himself took our infirmities and bare our sicknesses"* (Matthew 8:17). Jesus took my sickness so I do not have to bear my sickness any longer. Thus I can rise out of my sickness acting on the Word of God, which cannot fail. The Lord is my Healer!

The Four Steps of Faith

There are four steps in receiving a promise of God. **First, you must hear the promise.** It is impossible to have faith for something unless you have heard that it has been provided for. How could you have faith for a new pair of shoes when you were in your father's home unless he told you he was going to buy you a new pair of shoes? If he did not say that he would buy you a pair of shoes you could not have faith that you would receive them. You may hope that you will receive the shoes, but you don't have faith that you will. You could not have perfect faith for the shoes until your father promised them from his lips. Hope and faith are two different forces. Hope is always in the future, but faith is now. When you have faith for the shoes because of your father's promise, you see them (in your mind) already on your feet. You know your father's word is good and nothing will change his mind. His promise will produce the shoes.

You cannot have "unwavering faith" for some need that you have unless God has said that He would meet that need. You may have hope that He will meet your need, but you cannot have faith that He will. It is impossible to have faith until you have heard the promise to cover your need. It is not God's will that you hope for His healing. He wants you to have faith to actually believe for your healing because you have heard the promise that He heals.

The Word of God in the Bible is called "the Seed." The seed must be planted before the crop will grow. A farmer might say, "God, you are able to give me a crop of corn in my field even though I have not planted the corn seeds." Yes, God would be *able* to give the farmer a crop of corn before he planted his corn seed, but God is not *willing*. It is God's will after the seed has been planted, to give the farmer the crop of corn. God is able to save you, heal you, etc., even though you haven't planted the seed, the Word of God, to cover your needs. But He is not *willing*. God wants the seed, which is the promise, to be planted before He will save, provide or heal.

So the first step of faith is to plant the seed by hearing the Word of God.

Understanding the Word

The second step is to understand the promise. If you do not understand the promise in the Word of God, it is still of no use to you. Many times, through false teachings, traditions of men or pre-conceived ideas, we have failed to understand the promise contained in God's Word. And if we do not understand the promise, no matter how simple it is, we cannot have perfect faith. If, for any reason, we think God does not mean it to be for us, when He gives a promise in His Word, it would be impossible to exercise perfect faith. If you thought your earthly father was talking to your brother when he promised a new pair of shoes, you certainly could not have real faith to believe that you would receive the shoes. You must, after hearing the promise, be convinced that the promise is for you. You are to hear the promise and understand it.

Believing the Word

After you have heard and understood, **the third step is to believe the promise of God.** The promise will certainly do you no good if you do not believe it. The Bible speaks about people who hear the promise, but because they do not believe it, *"the devil taketh away the Word out of their hearts, lest they believe and be saved"* (Luke 8:12). There is nothing that grieves the heart of God any greater than when a Christian, a son of God, hears the Word, understands it, and yet does not believe it. There is nothing that would hurt an earthly father any greater than for his child to hear the promise of a new pair of shoes, but refuse to believe it, thus calling his father a liar. When we don't believe the Word once "light" has come our way, it is the same as telling God that you think He is a liar. The Bible says, *"God is not a man, that He can lie…"* (Numbers 23:19) It is impossible for God to lie. That alone should be enough to cause you to believe His Word.

Act on God's Word
The fourth and last step is to act on the Word of God. We can hear, understand and believe the promises in the Word of God, but if we do not act on them we have only "dead faith." When you act on the Word, God goes into action with you to fulfill His Word. It is not until you act on the Word, however, that God fulfills His Word. It is like carrying a check in your pocket. It is of no use to you until you go to the bank and demand your money. You are acting to fulfill the promise of these finances. The check will do you no good in your pocket. It alone will not put clothes on your back, or food in your stomach. But when you act on the check by cashing it, then your needs will be supplied through the money.

If you are still blind after the "prayer of faith," start looking. The deaf should start listening. The lame should start walking. The sick should get up out of their sick bed. This is acting on the Word of God. The Moffatt Translation of Matthew 7:24-27 says,

> *"Now every one who listens to these words of mine and acts upon them will be like a sensible man who built his house on rock. Down came the rain, floods rose, winds blew and beat upon that house, but it did not fall for it was founded upon the rock and everyone who listens to these words of mine and does not act upon them will be like a stupid man who built his house on the sand. Down came the rain, floods rose, winds blew and beat upon that house, till down it fell, and mighty was the crash."*
>
> –Matthew 7:24-27

In this Scripture we see how important it is to act on God's Word. If you will take this chapter and apply it to yourself you too will have the mountain-moving faith that God wants all His children to have.

> *"For verily I say unto you, If ye have faith as a grain of mustard seed, ye shall say unto this mountain, Remove hence to yonder place; and it shall remove; and nothing shall be impossible unto you."*
>
> –Matthew 17:20

> *"Jesus answered and said unto them, Verily I say unto you, If ye have faith, and doubt not, ye shall not only do this which is done to the fig tree, but also if ye shall say unto this mountain, Be thou removed, and be thou cast into the sea; it shall be done. 22 And all things, whatsoever ye shall ask in prayer, believing, ye shall receive."*
>
> –Matthew 21:21-22

During the healing meetings we held in the British Isles in those early days, we watched as people responded to the Word of God we were preaching. These four steps were evident in their response to my preaching. People would hear the Word and then they began to understand it. It was not long before we could tell they believed it and then they came forward to those altars in the town halls of Ireland to put their faith into action. Shouts and cries of joy filled those halls as the sick were healed and people laid hold of the promises of God for themselves.

Through these four steps—hearing, understanding, believing and acting, you too can move the mountains of worry, unbelief, lack, poverty, mental torment, and even life-threatening disease or sickness. You have the power of faith because God has *"dealt to every man the measure of faith"* (Romans 12:3). You can have all of God's promises fulfilled by putting your faith into action.

Summary

1. **God's Word is the title deed to whatever we need.**
2. **I must have more than hope—I must have faith.**
3. **I must take the four steps of faith.**

The Four Steps of Faith

1. Plant the seed by hearing the Word of God.
2. Understand the Promises of God.
3. Believe the Promises of God.
4. Act on the Word of God and receive your healing.

CHAPTER II

Is Your Sickness a Thorn in the Flesh?

And lest I should be exalted above measure by the abundance of the revelations, a thorn in the flesh was given to me, a messenger of Satan to buffet me, lest I be exalted above measure. Concerning this thing I pleaded with the Lord three times that it might depart from me.

–2 Corinthians 12:7-8

I can't remember how many people approached me after a healing service or after speaking to them in a prayer line who expressed the concept that they felt their sickness was like Paul's thorn in the flesh. One of the greatest excuses used by Christians, as well as the critics of divine healing, has been the biblical reference to Paul's thorn in the flesh. It is one of the most prevalent objections raised against the ministry of healing today.

But have you ever considered the fact that even "if" Paul's thorn was sickness (which it certainly was not), that should not keep you from being healed? Have you ever considered the hundreds of sick and suffering that were healed through the ministry of Paul? The Bible tells us in Acts 19:11, *"God wrought special miracles by the hands of Paul: so that from his body were brought unto the sick handkerchiefs or aprons, and the diseases departed from them, and the evil spirits went out of them."* None of the sick or diseased in Paul's day let Paul's thorn become an excuse for them to keep their sickness and diseases, so why should we let it be our excuse today?

In Matthew 9:35, it says, *"And Jesus went about all the cities and villages, teaching in their synagogues and preaching the Gospel of the Kingdom, and healing every sickness and every disease among the people."* Do you remember any place in the Bible telling of Jesus turning someone away and refusing to heal them because they had a thorn in their flesh? If He healed them, without any exceptions, He will heal us today, because *"He is the same yesterday, today and forever." "He forgiveth all thine iniquities; and healeth all thy diseases."* Notice the Word of God says "all" without any exceptions!

Paul very plainly tells us what his thorn in the flesh was, what it did, and why it was sent to him. In 2 Corinthians 12:7, it reads, *"And lest I should be exalted above measure through the abundance of the revelations there was given to me a thorn I the flesh, the messenger of Satan, to buffet me, lest I would be exalted above measure."*

The Thorn in Other Places in the Bible

The expression "thorn in the flesh" is not used in the entire Bible except as an illustration. Not one of these illustrations is used in pertaining to sickness. For example, in Numbers 33:35,

> *"But if ye will not drive out the inhabitants of the land from before you, then it shall come to pass that those which ye let remain of them shall be pricks in your eyes and thorns in your sides, and shall vex you in the land wherein ye dwell."*

We very definitely see that God is using the words *"thorns in your sides"* as an illustration of an enemy. Deuteronomy 7:15 declares, *"And the Lord will take away from thee all sickness."* Exodus 23:25 states, *"I will take sickness away from the midst of thee."* The Bible declares in Psalms that *"there was not one feeble person among them"* (Psalm 105:37).

The pricks in their eyes and the thorns in the sides of the children of Israel were the Canaanites! They were personalities! The Canaanites would be as thorns in the flesh if they were left in the land. It was an illustration and not something hooked to their flesh. How foolish it would be to think of a Canaanite protruding out of the side of the Israelites. Again in Joshua 23:13, *"They shall be as scourges in your sides and thorns in your eyes."* Again we see the expression *"thorn in the flesh"* speaking of personalities! It plainly tells us this thorn (the Canaanites) was a grievance to the children of Israel. The Bible is also very clear on Paul's thorn. We can fully understand its meaning if we will not close our minds or be bound by old ways of thinking, which are based on the traditions of men. Traditions bring a snare, but God's Word will make us free.

How could Paul have testified to the fact that he *"enjoyed the fullness of the blessing of the Gospel"* if he were sick, since healing is a definite part of the Gospel? There are those who claim Paul had sore eyes, yet they cannot find a single shred of truth for believing such. Bad eyes are one thing Paul could not have had, since God had healed him of blindness. In the ninth chapter of Acts, Paul's conversion is recorded. The light shone from heaven and a voice spoke. Upon arising from the ground where Paul had fallen, he was blind. For three days Paul neither ate nor drank. Then God spoke to Ananias to go and lay his hands on Paul and the Bible says, *"Immediately there fell from his eyes as it had been scales, and Paul received his sight."* Paul was healed of blindness!

> *"Brother Saul, the Lord, even Jesus, that appeared unto thee in the way as thou camest, hath sent me, that thou mightest receive thy sight, and be filled with the Holy Ghost. **18** And immediately there fell from his eyes as it had been scales: and he received sight forthwith, and arose, and was baptized."*
>
> –Acts 9:17-18

Healing was Part of Paul's Ministry

Healing is part of the gospel and Paul taught and demonstrated healing. Surely Paul believed and practiced Mark 16:17, *"And these signs shall follow them that believe, in My name shall they cast out devils, and they shall speak with new tongues, they shall take up serpents, if they drink any deadly thing it shall not hurt them, and they shall lay hands on the sick and they shall recover.*" These signs shall follow them that believe. Paul certainly was a believer, for he said much concerning the laying on of hands in his writings. He must have believed in healing, since so many were healed under his ministry.

"*In My name shall they cast out devils.*" Paul did that very thing. Acts 16:18 says, "*I command thee in the name of Jesus Christ to come out of her…and he (demon) came out of her.*"

"*They shall speak with new tongues.*" Paul believed this part too. In 1 Corinthians 14:18 he writes "*I speak in tongues more than ye all.*" Paul hasn't discredited any of Mark 16.

"*They shall take up serpents.*" Paul shook one from his hand, and those watching expected it to kill him, but it did him no harm (Acts 28:3).

"*And if they drink any deadly thing it shall not hurt them.*" In all of Paul's missionary journeys he must have drunk polluted or questionable water since most missionaries do.

And the most important part of Mark 16:18 declares, "*and they shall lay hands on the sick and they shall recover.*" Surely Paul believed in that portion of the verse since he so beautifully demonstrated it in his own ministry. If Paul were sick, would he not have laid his own hands on his own body? Those same hands that had been laid on others and brought healing could have been laid on his own body if he had been sick. Paul certainly taught and demonstrated his authority over sickness. Why would he have kept *his* sickness when he healed *others* from theirs? Why would he have tolerated disease in his own body when he reproved the Corinthians for being sick and even dying prematurely? If he were not a living example of his own teachings (and those of Christ), why would he have said, "*Be ye…followers of me*" (1 Corinthians 11:1; Philippians 3:17)?

After Jesus told His twelve disciples, in Mark 10, to go out and heal the sick and cast out devils, would we have expected to read in the Bible stories that the twelve disciples were confined at home with the flu, or in bed with pneumonia, or in a hospital dying with cancer?

Jesus also sent out seventy more to do the same—heal the sick and cast out devils. If they too had been sick, how could they have come back rejoicing, telling Jesus even the devils were subject to them in Jesus' name? They had been given authority and used it! They were instruments of healing and experienced the same!

Regardless of who was sick, they had power over that sickness. Would they not have used that same power to heal themselves, if they were sick? You would probably answer this question in the affirmative. Keep in mind that this was also long before Paul's time. Then in Mark 16, that same command with power was given to all believers everywhere. And since Christ is the same yesterday, today and forever, it would certainly have been operational in the Apostle Paul's ministry.

Not a Respecter of Persons

Since Christ is the same yesterday, today and forever and is no respecter of persons, Paul is included. We find that he not only believed in healing, but practiced it. That is exactly why Paul could encourage them to follow him. If Paul had not believed what Jesus said, we could not follow Paul into a victorious life. Yet we know that Paul's life was one of triumph! He said, *"Thanks be unto God, who always causes us to triumph through Christ our Lord"*(2 Corinthians 2:14).

And so, if Paul was following Christ, he followed Christ into health, since by those stripes laid on Jesus, Paul was healed. But on the other hand if Paul were sick, we should follow Paul into sickness, since he told us to follow him. That would be contrary to 3 John 2, *"Beloved, I wish above all things that thou mayest prosper and be in health, even as thy soul prospers."* There are no greater writings, nor more positive statements, neither can one find any more words of triumph greater than those Paul has penned. Yet Christians have interpreted Paul's thorn as sickness, and thus become content to tolerate illnesses in their own bodies, and thereby refuse to accept and embrace the won-

15

derful life-giving promises of our loving Heavenly Father, the Lord Who is our Healer!

Paul's Thorn Mysterious

Throughout the church age, Paul's thorn has been used as something "hidden" and mysterious, and the church has used it as a negative loophole to put up with sickness. Paul knew Jesus had said, *"Behold I give you power over all the power of the enemy,"* or simply, *"power over all sickness and disease."* If Paul knew he had this power would he have remained sick, as some believe he was, and then pen those wonderful words in Romans 8:37, *"We are more than conquerors"?* A sick person, in pain and weakness, doesn't feel like a conqueror, neither are they able to conquer.

Paul, himself, tells us exactly what his thorn was. He did not leave us in the dark concerning it. If we read the context for ourselves, we understand what the thorn was and note: sickness is the one thing not mentioned! 2 Corinthians 11:23-27 lists these things:

> *"in labors more abundant, in stripes above measure, in prisons more frequent, in deaths often, of the Jews five times received I forty stripes save one, thrice was I beaten with rods, once was I stoned, thrice I suffered shipwreck, a night and a day I have been in the deep; in journeyings often, in perils of waters, in perils of robbers, in perils by mine own countrymen, in perils by heathen, in perils in the city, in perils by the wilderness, in perils in the sea, in perils amongst false brethren; in weariness and painfulness, in watchings often, in hunger and thirst, in fastings often, in cold and nakedness."*

Traditions not always True to God's Word

One traditional idea has led to another, until the enemy, as far as Paul's thorn is concerned, has used this errant concept to become a hindrance to divine healing. Satan has distorted God's Word and blocked our healing through one single phrase that questions healing because of Paul's thorn. This is not meant as a slur to men and women or preachers and churches who have accepted this blinding tradition, but we must open our eyes to see how clever Satan has been in blinding the "very elect." Let us wake up and declare the whole counsel of God. Don't leave any foothold for Satan to use against us and against faith.

Paul has very definitely stated what his *"thorn in the flesh"* was, (2 Corinthians 12:7). He described it as a "messenger *of Satan,"* or a personality. So there need be no guessing or misunderstanding about it. The word "messenger" is translated from the Greek "angelos" which is always translated in the Bible as an angel or a messenger, or in other words, a personality. So this thorn was Satan's angel or his messenger. Naturally, coming from Satan, this angel would put undue pressure on Paul's life, which is recorded in this letter to the Corinthians, to let us know the many things with which Paul had to contend. Paul not only told us what the thorn in his flesh was (one of the devil's angels), but he tells us what this messenger came to do.

Satan Buffets Paul

Paul declares that this messenger of Satan was there to buffet him. 2 Corinthians 12:7 reads, *"There was given to me a thorn in the flesh, the messenger of the devil to buffet me..."* Buffet means to deal blow after blow. This satanic angel caused blow after blow upon Paul. If you will remember at the time Ananias came to Paul, when Paul's eyesight was restored, Paul was told he would suffer for the name of the Lord.

In addition to the persecutions mentioned in 2 Corinthians 11, the book of Acts records the Jews taking counsel to kill him, hindrances to his being accepted among the fellowship of Christians, opposition from Satan, opposition from the Jews, being expelled from Antioch, being stoned and left for dead, beaten and jailed, the many times he was mobbed and plotted against, and the many other hardships Paul endured. All this was in addition to the persecutions recorded in 2 Corinthians 11. We should note, with an open heart, almost everything but sickness is recorded in Paul's life. Yet, tradition claims the one thing Paul doesn't mention, and labels Paul's thorn as sickness! But why was this thorn not removed from Paul's life?

Paul had many accomplishments in his life for the Lord. Paul wrote more of the New Testament than any one person. Paul wrote about the revelation concerning the second coming of Jesus Christ.

> *"For the Lord Himself shall descend from heaven with a shout, with the voice of the Archangel, and the trump of God: and the dead in Christ shall rise first: then we which are alive and remain shall be caught up together with them in the clouds, to meet the Lord in the air, and so shall we ever be with the Lord."*
>
> —1 Thessalonians 4:16,17

Again Paul wrote in Corinthians concerning this mystery, *"For this corruptible must put on incorruption, and this mortal must put on immortality."* To Paul was also revealed the mystery concerning the Body of Christ, i.e. how we are all (regardless of denomination) members of the Body of Christ.

To Paul was given the revelation of *"Christ in you the hope of glory."* Paul unveils to us the workings of the Spirit, the gifts of the Spirit and the fruit of the Spirit. Paul was sent around the known world at that time to enlighten the Gentiles. Paul was a great preacher of truths because of the many revelations that were given him.

Maybe you have been keeping your sickness because you thought Paul's thorn was sickness. You knew he prayed three times for it to be removed, and it was not removed, so you thought you must be patient and bear your sickness, thinking your sickness was the thorn you must carry. If this is so, then you must accept the rest of the truth.

What is Your Excuse?

There is only one way you can be eligible to keep your so-called "thorn of sickness" and that must be the same reason Paul had for his thorn. 2 Corinthians 12:7 makes it clear,

> *"Lest I should be exalted above measure through the abundance of the revelations there was given to me a thorn in the flesh, the messenger of Satan to buffet me, lest I should be exalted above measure."*
>
> —2 Corinthians 12:7

In this one Scripture we have the reason given twice for the thorn not being removed. So unless, or until you too, have an abundance of revelations, you have no right to use Paul's thorn as the reason for keeping your illness!

If you claim your sickness is even as Paul's thorn, why don't you glory in your sickness? Paul said he took pleasure in infirmities. In other words, Paul gloried in his thorn. So why don't you glory in your sickness if you think it's your thorn? The very ones that say they believe this are often the first to go to a doctor to be relieved of their thorn. If a thorn of sickness would make a "Paul" out of some weak Christians, should they not seek sickness rather than healing? If your cancer is Paul's thorn, why go to the hospital and have it treated?

Paul's thorn never caused him to be inactive, for Paul said, *"I labored more abundantly than they all"* (1 Corinthians 15:10). Can a sick person do more than a well person? If Paul's *"thorn in the flesh"* was some type of sickness, or eye disease, etc., how could the cripple at Lystra receive faith to be healed by "seeing" and hearing Paul preach?

> *"And there sat a certain man at Lystra impotent in his feet, being a cripple from his mother's womb, who never had walked: the same heard Paul speak: who steadfastly beholding him, and perceiving that he had faith to be healed, said with a loud voice, stand upright on thy feet. And he leaped and walked."*
>
> —Acts 14:8-10

It would seem very hard to this cripple to muster up faith to be healed had Paul been standing before him sick or blind or diseased in his eyes. This is only one of the hundreds that were healed through the ministry of Paul. Certainly Paul was not sick!

So then we have found out by careful and open-minded study of God's Word that Paul's thorn was buffetings and persecutions caused by a messenger of Satan, because of his abundant revelations. Neither Paul nor God said the thorn was sickness, so why would we?

Summary

1. Paul's thorn was not sickness.
2. Paul had a ministry of healing and was healthy.
3. He never mentions being sick.
4. Paul's thorn was a personality, a messenger of Satan.
5. Paul's thorn was given to buffet him.
6. It buffeted him because of his abundant revelations.
7. Believers should not embrace sickness as a thorn to bear.

CHAPTER III

The Mystery of Job's Afflictions

So Satan answered the LORD and said, "Skin for skin! Yes, all that a man has he will give for his life. "But stretch out Your hand now, and touch his bone and his flesh, and he will surely curse You to Your face!" And the LORD said to Satan, "Behold, he is in your hand, but spare his life." So Satan went out from the presence of the LORD, and struck Job with painful boils from the sole of his foot to the crown of his head.

–Job 2:4-7

I recall one woman who actually believed that her affliction and sickness was given by God to teach her something. She said she felt like Job and that she just needed to suffer for awhile to learn these lessons from God. Obviously she could not be healed in our meetings. Many others we met had the same misconception.

This is another common argument against healing—the Bible story of Job's boils. It is perplexing how we tend to search for a way out of healing, rather than a way into healing. We will reach out and grasp tradition and hang onto Paul's thorn or Job's boils as an excuse for not believing for our healing, or as the reason we didn't receive it when someone prayed for us. But, like the children of Israel taking the promised land, we first have to dispossess before we can possess! We need to dispossess old reasoning from our minds—that reasoning that links us to the earthly realm through our five senses and balks at being educated in the faith realm.

Theories and Traditions

Let us keep our minds open, not to tradition, but to what God says in His Word. We should meditate in it day and night. And regardless of tradition, or old theories we may have depended on for years, let us open ourselves to the life- giving promises of God's Word. If God says differently than our old thoughts, we need to cast off our reliance on traditions and theories and accept His Word and His Word alone!

> *"Blessed is the man*
> *Who walks not in the counsel of the ungodly,*
> *Nor stands in the path of sinners,*
> *Nor sits in the seat of the scornful;*
> *But his delight is in the law of the LORD,*
> *And in His law he meditates day and night.*
> *He shall be like a tree*
> *Planted by the rivers of water,*
> *That brings forth its fruit in its season,*
> *Whose leaf also shall not wither;*
> *And whatever he does shall prosper."*
>
> –Psalms 1:1-3

Many times we were asked to go to a home and pray for someone that was ill but then faced the argument that just as Job had boils, these dear saints had reasoned themselves into being ill and keeping their illness. They believed that in some twisted way, God wanted them to be sick. You see, many sick people, in reality, do not want to be healed. They like to be waited on, and they thrive on sympathy. Therefore, they search for an excuse to keep their sickness. And other dear sick folk are eager to get rid of their sickness but because they have been taught the old theory, "be patient—remember Job," they remain in confusion, with their sickness, yet eager for deliverance.

Then there are those who come to our meetings for prayer and yet cannot be healed because of the mentality that hinders them from receiving their healing. Sometimes they waver when asked if they are ready to receive their healing. We often presume they are ready for healing. However, they sometimes answer, "Well, I don't know if God wants me to be healed. You know Job had boils and he was a perfect man, yet Job was sick." If they believed that, why come to be healed?

God cannot bless us with healing while there is doubt in our mind that He even wants to. Neither can we pray the prayer of faith if we are not sure God wills to heal now! How unfair it would be of God to tell us we can be healed and then keep our minds fogged with a negative question about Job's boils? It would become impossible to pray a prayer of faith.

The New Testament is straightforward about Jesus being willing to heal (Matthew 8:3) and healing all who came to Him (Matthew 9:35), healing every sickness and every disease among the people. But if God somehow wants to work something out in our lives by using sickness, as some describe Job's boils, then why didn't Jesus recognize such people during His ministry and tell them to be patient with their sickness? Jesus upset that argument by healing all who came to Him, and curing every disease they had!

You may say, as other sincere Christians have said, "Maybe I am God's Job." Yet, you probably have been seeking healing. Maybe you have been prayed for several times without results. The reason you are not healed may be that your healing is not clear in your own mind. You are not sure healing is for you, since in the back of your mind you have a doubt, thinking maybe you are like Job and need to suffer. On the other hand, why do you seek to be healed if you really believe God might want you to keep your sickness? That certainly would be working contrary to what you actually believe. But it is most certainly contrary to God's Word!

I encourage you to focus on studying the Bible story of Job in order to seek a clear understanding from God's Word on this matter of faith. We have a right to know what is in God's Word since it is for us. His Word is the record of His promises to us—our promised land to possess. His commandments are not hard and His Word is not complicated. We would not appreciate receiving a letter from someone that was so complex we could not understand. Neither do we believe God would write to us and make it so complicated that we cannot understand it.

Before the Stripes of Calvary

Job lived on the other side of the cross—before stripes were laid on the back of Jesus for our healing. We should note that the Book of Job was written before the covenant of healing was given. Job lived in another era, even before the Law.

While the Bible says Job was a perfect man, we may have misinterpreted the meaning of that word. It does not mean sinless perfection. The Bible tells us "all have sinned" (Romans 3:23). As New Testament believers, we recognize our perfection is in Christ.

Job loved the Lord and grew into godly maturity by seeking to live as a God pleaser. He loved and desired God with all his heart. Yet even Job, in his hunger to walk with God, was a man subject to pride. In Elihu's conversation with Job, he begins the first verse of the 33rd chapter with these words, *"Wherefore, Job, I pray thee, hear my speeches, and hearken to all my words."* Then in the same chapter and the 17th verse, Elihu says, *"That he may withdraw man from his purpose, and hide pride from man."* A friend is said to be one who knows all our faults and loves us in spite of them. It sometimes takes a rude awakening, through a friend, to cause us to come face-to-face with our weaknesses.

Self Righteousness

Job was righteous, but perhaps most of all in his own eyes. The Bible says, *"Our (own) righteousness is as filthy rags"* (Isaiah 64:6). There was a spiritual pride Job had apparently acquired. For the many "Jobs" who believe they are suffering for righteousness' sake, and have become spiritual martyrs of a sort, God has already said we have no righteousness of our own, and thus they should turn from it! The only possible righteousness we can attain is self righteousness! That self righteousness will certainly hinder our healing. Until we get our eyes off ourselves and onto Christ, and know it is only His righteousness we have, we are clogging the channel for our healing with rags of self righteousness.

Satan is a Liar

Perhaps we have sat down in the midst of our illness, resigned to the thought that we were suffering even as Job, because it was for God's glory. Yet it is with haste we might still call a doctor to take away "Job's sickness" when the pain gets too severe, or if it looks serious. Then we are anxious to get rid of our sickness, Job or no Job! We forget all about the glory God is supposedly getting from our illness, or the patience He is working out in our life through it. How quickly we change our minds when the doctor's diagnosis is a life-threatening disease.

In the first place, we should draw our attention to the fact that the devil (not God) made Job sick! God said to Satan, *"He is in your hand"* (Job 2:6). Satan, not God, put these things upon Job. If you are seeking healing, it is important that you fully realize that your illness has come from Satan's hand, not from God's! That truth makes us want to immediately get rid of sickness. God has only one part in our sickness—that of healing us from it!

We cannot think defeat and obtain victory. Job's first mistake was his mind. *"Out of the abundance of the heart the mouth speaks"* (Matthew 12:34). When Job uttered the words, *"The thing which I greatly feared is come upon me,"* (Job 3:25), he voiced what was in his heart. This fear was not faith. Hidden inside, in spite of the outward appearance of calm, was a spirit of fear.

Fear Opens the Door to Trouble

Fear and faith are like oil and water—they will not mix. When we believe, it puts God into action! When we fear, we are signing a receipt for Satan to come in with disaster! Job signed the receipt for Satan to come in when he dipped his pen into the ink of fear, and wrote it across his own heart!

Fear is not trust! Fear is not from God because *"fear hath torment"* (1 John 4:18). God does not want His own people to be tormented with fear. He cushions us from the strain of fear and speaks to our hearts so tenderly, these words, *"Lo, I am with you always!"* Can the shadows remain where the sun shines so bright? Can the darkness of fear remain when the Sun of Righteousness lights our pathway? Cast aside every doubt, every fear, lest Satan gain any advantage. We are not in bondage to Satan. Satan is in bondage to the believer! Learn to refuse fear and it will have no power over you. Remember, fear was Job's way of opening his life to Satan's workings! Fear was Job's first downfall.

You may have heard the expression, "I had my dreams realized." But Job had his fears realized. When Job said, *"The thing I feared is come upon me,"* he signed a legal document for Satan to come in and attack!

Satan is the Author of Fear

Fear is one of evil's most potent forces! God wants us to *"fear no evil, for He is with (us)"* (Psalm 23:4). Satan's powers of evil watch us with our weak spots as their target. They attack our vulnerable areas attempting to tear down love (but perfect love will cast out fear). If we tolerate fear, it allows Satan to have an unhindered entrance.

Fear the future? No, Jesus will be with you!
Fear poverty? No, Jesus will provide!
Fear sickness? No, Jesus is your healer!
Fear whispers that God might fail you.
Fear only has power over you as you place yourself under it!
Fight fear as you would fight a plague!
Depression is a state of fear! Fight depression! Depression is the impression left by fear!
Love and fear cannot dwell together!

Faith and worry live apart, but love and faith walk in harmony together!

Fear will not bring healing, but faith will!

Remember, the thing Job feared came upon him.

On the other hand, Job did have faith. He trusted God to deliver him. Job took no medicine and did not lean on the arm of flesh (Jeremiah 17:4). If you want to be like Job, why then do you seek a doctor's help? If you are God's Job, why not trust God? Job said, *"though He slay me, yet will I trust in Him"* (Job 13:15).

The fact is that Job was made sick by Satan. But God healed him! Job did not remain sick! God was not in Job's sickness—God was in his deliverance! And God Almighty is not in your sickness—He is in your healing! There may be many remedies, but there is only one cure—and that is Christ!

The Cause of Job's Affliction

The devil sought to destroy Job. God did not cause this nor was He trying to teach Job a lesson. No, it was simply an attack of an enemy. The devil was testing and tempting Job through sickness and trouble, yet the Lord turned it around for good in the end as He always does and as He will for you!

> *"And we know that all things work together for good to them that love God, to them who are the called according to his purpose".*
>
> —Romans 8:28

You can be sure that the same Lord who delivered Job out of His afflictions will deliver you. *"Many are the afflictions of the righteous, but the Lord delivers him out of them all"* (Psalm 34:19). God delivered Job out of all his troubles. God didn't start this but He did end it! He didn't cause it, but He did solve it! He didn't bring it on Job, but He did lift it off him! Quit applying your sickness to God. Go ahead and blame the devil and then resist him and be healed!

"Submit yourselves therefore to God. Resist the devil, and he will flee from you."

–James 4:7

"Be sober, be vigilant; because your adversary the devil, as a roaring lion, walketh about, seeking whom he may devour: [9] Whom resist stedfast in the faith, knowing that the same afflictions are accomplished in your brethren that are in the world."

–1 Peter 5:8-9

"For this purpose the Son of God was manifested, that he might destroy the works of the devil."

–1 John 3:8

"That through death he might destroy him that had the power of death, that is, the devil;"

–Hebrews 2:14

"And ought not this woman, being a daughter of Abraham, whom Satan hath bound, lo, these eighteen years, be loosed from this bond on the sabbath day?"

–Luke 13:16

"God anointed Jesus of Nazareth with the Holy Ghost and with power: who went about doing good, and healing all that were oppressed of the devil; for God was with him."

–Acts 10:38

"So the servants of the householder came and said unto him, Sir, didst not thou sow good seed in thy field? from whence then hath it tares? [28] He said unto them, An enemy hath done this."

–Matthew 13:27-28

"And the great dragon was cast out, that old serpent, called the Devil, and Satan, which deceiveth the whole world: he was cast out into the earth, and his angels were cast out with him. ¹⁰ And I heard a loud voice saying in heaven, Now is come salvation, and strength, and the kingdom of our God, and the power of his Christ: for the accuser of our brethren is cast down, which accused them before our God day and night. ¹¹ And they overcame him by the blood of the Lamb, and by the word of their testimony; and they loved not their lives unto the death."

–Revelation 12:9-11

The end result of the life of Job is a glorious one. If you want to claim something from the life of Job, claim this. Yes he suffered, but he lived 140 years and prospered twice as much in the end of his life as he did in the beginning. We don't know for sure, since the Bible doesn't tell us, but perhaps Job's suffering and trouble lasted only a few months or even for a few years. But compared to 140+ years of prosperity and blessing, a short time of suffering is nothing. No matter what you may be going through, know for sure that the Lord who delivered the man of God, Job, will deliver you.

"For which cause we faint not; but though our outward man perish, yet the inward man is renewed day by day. ¹⁷ For our light affliction, which is but for a moment, worketh for us a far more exceeding and eternal weight of glory; ¹⁸ While we look not at the things which are seen, but at the things which are not seen: for the things which are seen are temporal; but the things which are not seen are eternal."

–2 Corinthians 4:16-18

God who works all things together for good (Romans 8:28) will surely work this out for your good as well. He doesn't initiate evil or cause bad things to happen in our lives, but He does resolve them and change them and cause them to work for our benefit. What the devil meant for evil, God intended for good (Genesis 50:20). This affliction is light. This suffering is temporary. This difficulty is just for a moment. But the resulting glory will be forever.

Summary

1. The traditions of men have taught that Job was afflicted because God was teaching him something.
2. Job was afflicted with sickness by the devil, not God.
3. Job lived before the cross and was not perfect in that respect.
4. Job struggled with self righteousness, instead of true godly righteousness.
5. Job allowed Satan to attack because of a spirit of fear.
6. Job did believe God and trusted God to deliver him.
7. Job suffered briefly but was healed and delivered.
8. Job prospered twice as much in his latter days as in his former.

CHAPTER IV

Healing in the Atonement

Surely He has borne our griefs
And carried our sorrows;
Yet we esteemed Him stricken,
Smitten by God, and afflicted.
But He was wounded for our transgressions,
He was bruised for our iniquities;
The chastisement for our peace was upon Him,
And by His stripes we are healed.

—Isaiah 53:4-5

One evangelist was preaching healing when a woman came to him at the end of the service wanting to be healed of her affliction. She had come to many of the special healing meetings and was in the prayer lines, but could never get healed. The man of God was preaching about the cross of Jesus, declaring that healing was in the work of the atonement—that Jesus died not only for our sins, but also for our sicknesses. That night she came forward again and said, "Preacher, I never saw that in the Bible before. Now I know the Lord will heal me. You pray for me. I'm ready to receive my healing." And he did, and she did, that very moment.

The question of faith always rests on knowing the will of God. It is impossible to exercise perfect faith until the will of God is known. If you want healing for your body, then the first step is to find out the will of God concerning your body. We are to ask *"according to His will,"* and then we shall receive (1 John 5:14). To *"ask anything according to His will"* doesn't mean to guess about it. Many Christians believe that to ask according to His will is to pray—"If it be Thy will…" This unbiblical phrase is not asking according to His will, but rather guessing about it. The secret of faith is to know the will of God.

God's Desires Made Possible

One healing evangelist often said that 80% of getting healed is in believing it is the will of God to heal you. In 3 John 1:2, God makes it very clear what His desires are concerning your body. *"Beloved I wish above all things that thou mayest prosper and be in health, even as your soul prospereth."* This is God's highest desire for you, His son or daughter. It is God's wish that you and I be in health. God has made every provision for us to be healed so we can be in health. That healing has been provided through the atoning work of Jesus Christ.

Sickness and disease came upon the human race through sin. There was no sickness or disease in the Garden of Eden. God's first creation enjoyed health for the body, the soul and the spirit. Because of Adam's sin, death came upon man. *"By one man sin entered into the world, and death by sin…"* (Romans 5:12). The main causes of death to our bodies are sickness and disease. Sickness, disease and death have come upon the human race through sin, which Satan has caused. When Jesus was on earth he *"healed all who were oppressed of the Devil"* (Acts 10:38). Sickness and disease is a destructive force, but Jesus came to give life. *"For the Son of man is not come to destroy men's lives, but to save them"* (Luke 9:56).

Jesus Christ Delivered us from the Curse

Sickness was a curse that came upon man for his disobedience. God calls sickness and disease the *"curse of the law"* (Galatians 3:13). But *"Christ hath redeemed us from the curse of the law, being made a curse for us: for it is written, cursed is everyone that hangeth on a tree."* Christ has redeemed us from every curse.

What all is under the curse? The 28th chapter of Deuteronomy tells us the following things under the curse of the Law: *"consumption* (or tuberculosis), *fever, pestilence, inflammation, burning, botch, emrods, scab, itch, blindness, smiting of the knees and legs, failing of the eyes, madness."* And also in verses 60 and 61, *"All diseases…also every sickness and every plague, which is not written in this book…"* is under the curse of the law.

But, thank God, Christ has redeemed us from the curse of the law, which is sickness and disease. The word redeemed means—"to buy back, to be restored to the original state." To be redeemed means you and I have been restored to our original state. As Adam enjoyed health so should every redeemed child of God be in health.

"For ye are bought with a price: therefore glorify God in your body, and in your spirit, which are God's" (1 Corinthians 6:20). Your body is bought with a price or redeemed just as your spirit is redeemed. Your spirit, soul and body (after you are saved) now belong to God. Jesus was made a curse for us that we might be free from the curse. *"Himself took our infirmities, and bare our sickness" (Matthew 8:17). "Who His own self bare our sins…"* (1 Peter 2:27). Jesus not only redeemed us from our sins by bearing our sins for us, but He also redeemed us from our sickness by bearing our sicknesses for us. The prophet Isaiah declares, *"Surely He hath borne our griefs (*sickness), *and carried our sorrows* (pains*)"* (Isaiah 53:8). Christ has borne our sickness and disease, and has redeemed us from the curse of the law. Through the blood of Christ we have the *"forgiveness of sins"* (Ephesians 1:7). And *"by (His) stripes ye were healed"* (1 Peter 2:24).

Healing is in God's Plan of Atonement and Salvation

Healing was provided for in the atonement and the work of the Cross. Jesus not only died for our sins but also for our sicknesses. This primary doctrine and truth of God's Word is repeated and verified by three different writers and revealed in three major passages of Scripture. From the prophet Isaiah to the Gospel author Matthew, to the apostle Peter himself, this reality of what Jesus did in the work of redemption is clearly delineated. Both Old and New Testaments describe this primary doctrine.

Isaiah's prophecy

> *"Surely He has borne our griefs and carried our sorrows; Yet we esteemed Him stricken, Smitten by God, and afflicted. But He was wounded for our transgressions, He was bruised for our iniquities; The chastisement for our peace was upon Him, And by His stripes we are healed."*
>
> –Isaiah 53:4-5

> *"Surely our sicknesses he hath borne, And our pains--he hath carried them, And we--we have esteemed him plagued, Smitten of God, and afflicted."*
>
> –Isaiah 53:4 (Young's Literal Translation)

The Gospel of Matthew gives us a New Testament interpretation of Isaiah's prophecy. Matthew writes that this prophecy was fulfilled in the ministry of Jesus as He healed those who were sick.

> *"that it might be fulfilled which was spoken by Isaiah the prophet, saying: 'He Himself took our infirmities And bore our sicknesses.'"*
>
> –Matthew 8:17

> *"This was to fulfill what was spoken through the prophet Isaiah: 'He took up our infirmities and carried our diseases.'"*
>
> –Matthew 8:17 (NIV)

> *"that it might be fulfilled that was spoken through Isaiah the prophet, saying, 'Himself took our infirmities, and the sicknesses he did bear.'"*
>
> –Matthew 8:17 (Young's Literal Translation)

The apostle Peter also adds to this revelation and quotes Isaiah, reminding us that we were healed by the stripes of Jesus. Peter, of course, is looking back at the cross after it occurred and stating what Jesus did for all of us who believe when He died on the cross on our behalf. Isaiah said, *"by His stripes we are healed."* But the apostle Peter, writing his epistle after the resurrection of Christ from the dead, declares, *"by whose stripes you were healed"!*

> *"Who Himself bore our sins in His own body on the tree, that we, having died to sins, might live for righteousness--by whose stripes you were healed."*
>
> −1 Peter 2:24

> *"...by his wounds you have been healed"*
>
> −1 Peter 2:24 (NIV)

> *"...You have been healed by his wounds!"*
>
> −1 Peter 2:24 (NLT)

Healing is as much in the atonement as is forgiveness. That is why David declares in Psalms 103:2-3, *"Bless the Lord O my soul, and forget not all his benefits: who forgiveth all thine iniquities: who healeth all thy diseases..."* One of the great benefits of Calvary is supernatural healing for our bodies so we can be in health as God desires us to be.

We had countless numbers of people who were both saved and healed in the same service during those days of healing campaigns. It would happen over and over. I would always give an altar call for salvation first before praying for the sick. And most of those folks who came forward for salvation stayed right near the front to be prayed for to receive healing as well. Usually the people who were being saved, and had their hearts already opened by the Holy Spirit for forgiveness, readily accepted Jesus as their Healer also and received healing.

If you are a believer in Jesus, you can be confident in coming to Him for your healing, for He has made provision for your healing through His atoning work on the cross. When Jesus Christ died on the cross, He carried your sicknesses as well as your sins. Our diseases were nailed to that tree as well as our iniquities. Not only did our Heavenly Father judge the transgressions and sins of the world when His Son was crucified, He also dealt a death blow to illness and disease. Healing for every sickness known or unknown to man was provided for by the death of Jesus on the cross of Calvary. Jesus Christ is *"the same yesterday, today and forever"*, and if He *"healed all those who were sick"* in His day, He will do it in our day. If He did it for them, He will do it for you!

Summary

1. We don't pray "If it be Thy will...".
2. We know it is the will of God to heal us.
3. Sickness was a curse that came upon man for his disobedience.
4. Jesus has delivered us from the curse.
5. Healing is as much a part of the atonement as forgiveness.

CHAPTER V

Faith in the God of Healing

> *"So ought not this woman, being a daughter of Abraham,*
> *whom Satan has bound—think of it—for eighteen years,*
> *be loosed from this bond on the Sabbath?"*
>
> —Luke 13:11-16

Over the years we have prayed for many sick people laying on beds of sickness in hospitals. Many of those who were believers were healed and the Lord raised them up. All those with faith gladly received our prayers. But the saddest cases were people who somehow got a hold of a twisted concept of God and thought that God had put the sickness on them. They became bitter and even mad at God. Not only did they not receive healing, but they died in their bitterness and resentment. Sometimes relatives stood around them cursing God as their loved one passed into eternity.

But God is not to blame for sickness. He is not the god of sickness, but He is the God of healing. Do we understand how sickness entered this world? Romans 5:15 gives us the answer, *"Wherefore, as by one man sin entered into the world, and death by sin; and so death* (both spiritual and physical) *passed upon all men, for that all have sinned."*

According to the Bible, physical death, and all that is produced in connection with physical death, such as sickness, disease, etc. are the direct results of sin! Of course Satan is the originator of sin; therefore Satan is the source of sickness, in the same way as he is the source of sin. Satan is the *"god of this world"* (2 Cor. 4:4) and he is also the god of your sickness. Sin and sickness are very closely linked together. It was King David who had this revelation, writing about the Lord Who *"forgiveth all thine iniquities* (and) *who healeth all they diseases…"* (Psalms 103:3).

Power to Forgive, Power to Heal

Now we can understand Jesus' word in Mark 2:9, *"Whether is it easier to say to the sick of the palsy, thy sins be forgiven thee; or to say arise and take up thy bed and walk?"* People would not accept the truth that Jesus had power to forgive sin, so Jesus was telling them in so many words that He was going to prove that He had power to forgive this man's sin by healing him of his palsy! He was using words to this effect, "When you see that I can cure this sin-produced disease, you will certainly know that I am also able to take away sin itself!"

Jesus came into the world to accomplish man's redemption! He died and rose again, ascending to heaven, where He sat down at the right hand of God. But, before He sat down He finished the work He was sent into the world to do. *"For this purpose the Son of God was manifested that He might destroy the works of the devil"* (1 John 3:8). Christ died to destroy Satan's power over man. Hebrews 2:14 tells us, *"forasmuch then as the children are partakers of flesh and blood, He also Himself likewise took part of the same; that through death He might destroy him that had the power of death, that is the devil."* Christ died then, to destroy Satan's power over death. Is it not a fact that Satan uses sickness to cause death? But here in Hebrews we find that Christ died for the very reason of destroying the power of sickness! Jesus came not to destroy men's lives, but to save them. Satan destroys, but Jesus gives life!

We often have over-spiritualized the Word of God until His promises have no effect upon our bodies. If Satan cannot get us to dis-believe God, he will get us to spiritualize everything.

God's Desire for You to be in Health

It is today, and now, that we need help both spiritually and physically. We all agree that when we get to heaven we will have fully healthy bodies, free from any pain or sickness. But Jesus said in that wonderful, revealing prayer He taught His disciples in Matthew 6:10, *"Thy will be done in earth, as it is in Heaven!"* According to that Scripture, if God intends for us to have well bodies in the hereafter, then He wills for us to be well now, on the earth! *"Beloved, I wish above all things that thou mayest prosper and be in health, even as they soul prospereth"* (3 John 3).

As Christians, we have somehow shied away from the idea that sickness is from Satan. Had we remembered what God said about sickness and sin, classifying both from Satan, then remembering that Jesus took care of both in the atonement, we would be more confident about getting rid of our sickness. Your sickness came through Satan! But, it will leave through faith in Christ!

While we may have used nice dressed-up, modern medical terms for our diseases and our sicknesses, Jesus called them by their right name. And at the same time He let us know where the sickness originated.

Probably today we would describe the condition of the woman bowed over in Luke 13 as an arthritic condition or a stroke. We would probably not even mention the devil. But Jesus said in verse 16, *"Satan hath bound her,"* and when He loosed her from this *"spirit of infirmity,"* she immediately straightened up and was made whole!

There was another case of one possessed with a devil, blind and dumb (Matthew 12:22). When the devil was cast out, the blind eyes were opened and the dumb spoke! Thus it proved the hindering force was Satan and certainly not God, because the power of God loosed this one from Satan's hold.

How can I be Healed Now?

There is only one way to be healed and, of course, that is through faith in Christ's finished work. Most believers know the *what,* but they question the *how.* "How will God heal me?" The sick need only one thing to be perfectly healed—that is faith! Faith is the entire basis for healing. Faith in the finished work of Jesus is the key to receiving your healing. Before He sat down at the right hand of the Father, Jesus completed the work God sent Him to do. He completely redeemed us from sin and all its effects! Think of it! We are redeemed spiritually and physically! No wonder then the Psalmist says in one breath, *"Who forgiveth all thine iniquities; who healeth all thy diseases."* Our healing comes through believing this. The truth is, you are redeemed right now from sin and all that sin produces.

Satan has caused people to look at the word *faith* in such a complicated manner that it has looked like a mountain of impossibility. Let us use a simple word for faith, and without changing its meaning, help us grasp it more readily. Substitute confidence wherever you find the word faith. "Have confidence in God" (Mark 11:22). Actually that is all faith is, confidence that God said exactly what He meant and meant exactly what He said! Satan has deceived the Christian and made it seem hard to believe.

So then, faith, or confidence, is just believing exactly what God says. If I were to offer you a free book for the asking, you would simply ask me for the book. God has said in His Word there is healing for you in the stripes of Jesus. So we merely take Him at His word! What a wonderful thing faith is! What a privilege we have to show God we have complete confidence in Him.

Cross Over the Bridge

How tragic it would be to pass through this world without confidence in others, or without confidence in things in the natural. We would be most miserable. We could not go for a pleasure drive in the country if we did not have confidence. What if we came to the first bridge across a mountain stream, stopped the car and worried that maybe it wasn't really a bridge at all. Perhaps we refused to pass over the bridge and sat waiting until some other car came to cross over and test the bridge. We might even say, "Well, it held them up, but I still don't think it will hold me, it's about to go down, and it might go down with me." As foolish as it may seem, this is what we do with God many times. He has said in Exodus 23:25, *"I will take away sick-*

ness from the midst of thee." And again in Exodus 15:26, *"I am (present tense) the Lord that healeth thee."*

We come to the great bridge of God's Word, but we question it. *"He sent His Word and healed them"* (Psalms 107:20). The bridge, the Word of God, is safer than any natural bridge, and it will carry you across to victory!

> *"Hath He not spoken and shall He not make it good?"*
> —Numbers 23:19

> *"There hath not failed one word of all His good promises...!"*
> —1 Kings 5:58

> *"Faith without works is dead"*
> —James 2:20

Cross over the bridge! If you have confidence that God Almighty is back of His Word, then act on it and act in faith!

> *"And when Abram was ninety years old and nine, the LORD appeared to Abram, and said unto him, I am the Almighty God (El Shaddai); walk before me, and be thou perfect."*
> —Genesis 17:1

> *"Ah Lord GOD! behold, thou hast made the heaven and the earth by thy great power and stretched out arm, and there is nothing too hard for thee:"*
> —Jeremiah 32:17

> *"For with God nothing shall be impossible."*
> —Luke 1:37

> *"And he said, The things which are impossible with men are possible with God."*
> —Luke 18:27

"Fear not, Abram: I am thy shield, and thy exceeding great reward."

                                                                    –Genesis 15:1

"But without faith it is impossible to please him: for he that cometh to God must believe that he is, and that he is a rewarder of them that diligently seek him."

                                                                    –Hebrews 11:6

"Have not I written to thee excellent things in counsels and knowledge, 21 That I might make thee know the certainty of the words of truth; that thou mightest answer the words of truth to them that send unto thee?"

                                                                    –Proverbs 22:20-21

"And Peter answered him and said, Lord, if it be thou, bid me come unto thee on the water. 29 And he said, Come. And when Peter was come down out of the ship, he walked on the water, to go to Jesus."

                                                                    –Matthew 14:28-29

His Word is the basis for our faith, and that is the kind of faith, or confidence, that will cause us to become free from our pain and our sickness. *"He was wounded for our transgressions, He was bruised for our iniquities; the chastisement of our peace was upon Him: and with His stripes we are (now) healed"* (Isaiah 53:5).

The true disciple of Jesus believes to see, but the ordinary person twists that truth (like Thomas) and must see to believe. But God's abundant life does not work that way. There are those who are sincere, but wrong, in having the idea that if they live a good life, God will heal them. But that would be healing by our "works." God only moves in the channel of faith! If we receive anything from God through our own efforts, we would lower the sacrifices of Christ to the level of "works" and *"it is not by works lest any man boast"* (Ephesians 2:9). We were saved *"by grace* (God's power) *through faith* (our confident response)."

"For by grace are ye saved through faith; and that not of your-selves: it is the gift of God. Not of works, lest any man should boast"

–Ephesians 2:8-9

So in the same way we were saved, we are to walk out our faith. We were not saved by our works, and thus we cannot be healed by our works. No one qualifies to be healed. Jesus healed all who came to him. He healed the sinner and the saint. He healed the rich and the poor. He healed the prostitute and the Pharisee. He healed the young and the old. And no doubt He healed those who were good and some who were not.

"As ye have therefore received Christ Jesus the Lord, so walk ye in him"

–Colossians 2:6

So we are thus healed in the same way we were saved—*"by grace through faith."* We are healed by the power of God (grace) as we believe and have confidence (faith) in what He has promised! In fact, the entire plan of salvation, as revealed under the new covenant and ministry of Jesus is based on justification by faith and not by works.

"Knowing that a man is not justified by the works of the law, but by the faith of Jesus Christ, even we have believed in Jesus Christ, that we might be justified by the faith of Christ, and not by the works of the law: for by the works of the law shall no flesh be justified"

—Galatians 2:16

If we were justified or saved by faith and not by works, then it is equally true that we are healed by faith also, and not by our works. Jesus forgave our sins because we believed. In the same way, Jesus heals our sickness because we believe. Those who seek healing should not do so based on their merit or their good works. But rather, we should simply seek healing by faith regardless of whether or not we feel we deserve it.

When You Pray

When (according to Mark 11:24) are you to believe that you are healed? You are healed the moment prayer is made! *"When you pray, believe that ye shall receive, and you shall…!"*

Many times the full manifestation of a healing is not seen at the moment prayer is offered. However, we have never seen it to fail, that if a person will believe when they are prayed for, even though they may have to wait a while for the outcome, the results always follow. Though there might be delay in actually seeing our healing, it never means God has denied us. So often we void the healing prayer with our unbelief during the "waiting" season. Tradition says "if you were healed—you would feel like it," and our symptoms might even agree with tradition. But because we do not see or feel different, we are prone to cast aside God's Word which says, *"by whose stripes ye were healed."* Beware of faith-destroying words like, "I guess I'm not healed, I don't feel any different."

When we are prayed for, whether we pray for ourselves, or have another pray for our healing, we need to have confidence and believe! When should we believe? When we are prayed for! Bring it to a specific time. Make a point of contact! Pinpoint your believing!

Don't Stop Your Believing

The Bible tells us in Mark 11:24 (from the lips of Jesus), *"What things soever ye desire, when ye pray, believe that ye receive them, and ye shall have them."* As Christians we have much to learn along the line of patience. Our impatience often causes us to lose the answer to our prayer. But delay is not denial.

"Cast not away therefore your confidence, which hath great recompense of reward. For ye have need of patience, that, after ye have done the will of God, ye might receive the promise" (Hebrews 10:35-36). In other words, don't give up faith that you are healed and thereby lose the healing that

would be manifest in your body. Even though you may have to wait, maintain your confidence in God's promise. You are in God's will to seek your healing, because it is His will to heal you!

Sarah bore a son, *"Because she judged Him faithful who had promised"* (Hebrews 11:10). The moment the promise was given concerning this son, it was enough to start Sarah and Abraham believing it. They talked it! They could see it! They planned for it! In spite of natural conditions growing more and more impossible with the passing years, they had confidence in God's Word and He had promised them a son! Though Sarah's womb was now dead, and it seemed naturally impossible to bear a child, that did not hinder God's promise from coming to pass.

Faith sees no barriers! Faith knows no defeat! Faith refuses to make null and void the Word of God by looking through natural eyes. Faith holds on to *"thus saith the Lord."* And faith confesses what God says, not what circumstances might say!

> *"Our faith, that is the conquest which conquers the world"*
> —1 John 5:4 (Moffatt)

Positive Praise

You will find that if you repent of any negative talk and move into a positive confession, you will be amazed how circumstances will change! Talk God's language! Speak God's Word! Quote Bible verses! Pray the Scriptures! Can we even conceive of God speaking negatively? Then why do we? We are born into His family, bear His image and take on the attributes of our Heavenly Father. So we should speak His language. Amos 3:3 says, *"How can two walk together unless they be agreed."* How can we, as God's children, walk with Him unless we agree with Him?

> *"But thou art holy, O thou that inhabitest the praises of Israel."*
>
> —Psalms 22:3

"In every thing give thanks: for this is the will of God in Christ Jesus concerning you."

−1 Thessalonians 5:18

Remember, God inhabits the praises of His people. The Lord will not withdraw His healing from you. So after you receive prayer for healing, let the span between the offered prayer and your manifest healing be a time of praise and thanksgiving! It will surprise you to find how quickly your healing is completed. While praising God, it leaves little room for doubt to creep in. Praise and thanksgiving leave no time for gossip or condemnation or things that kill the spirit. Praise keeps the channel of faith clear and open! God inhabits your praises and where He is, there is healing!

Summary

1. **Satan is the source of sickness.**
2. **He causes both sin and sickness.**
3. **Satan is the god of your sickness.**
4. **God provides forgiveness for sin, and healing for sickness.**
5. **Cross over the bridge of faith.**
6. **We are healed in the same way we are saved.**
7. **When we pray, we should pray in faith.**
8. **Repent of negative attitudes and praise God for your healing.**

CHAPTER VI

Words of Power

"The word is near you, in your mouth and in your heart" (that is, the word of faith which we preach): that if you confess with your mouth the Lord Jesus and believe in your heart that God has raised Him from the dead, you will be saved. For with the heart one believes unto righteousness, and with the mouth confession is made unto salvation."

–Romans 10:8-10

Some of the saddest stories we heard after our healing meetings would be those of people who talked themselves out of their own healing. Even though they had been healed in our meetings, they wavered in their faith afterward, began looking at their symptoms and started talking like a foolish person. Their own words condemned them and robbed them of what God was trying to provide. They literally talked themselves out of being healed.

Our words during the waiting period, for a full manifestation of healing, are of tremendous importance. Words have influence. Words are always creative! Words build faith or they destroy faith. It is so easy to just talk without thinking and confess foolish things, but we have to realize the great value and consequence of words. Words can add to us, or words can rob us! Words create life or they create death.

Words, good or bad, will either hinder or help those who hear them. Words will cause life or death. Jesus said, *"The words that I speak unto you, they are spirit, and they are life"* (John 6:63). Can we say the same thing about our words? We often take so little thought about the words that come forth from our mouths. We use frivolous or shallow words to express our opinions and beliefs. The world, our neighbors, our friends, our family, and others only know us by our words. If a man's word is no good, he is considered no good. We judge one another by our words.

> *"out of the abundance of the heart the mouth speaketh"*
> —Matthew 12:34

> *"with the heart man believeth unto righteousness; and with the mouth confession is made unto salvation."*
> —Romans 10:10

In other words, whatever we really believe in our heart, our mouth will speak. How little importance we often put on our words? We use them so carelessly. Wise King Solomon declared in Proverbs 6:2, *"Thou art snared with the words of thy mouth, thou art taken with the words of thy mouth."* Not only are we snared with our words, but we open a door to the working of the devil through our words. Satan is looking for a door to our spirit, our soul, or our body, and our own mouth is one of Satan's main entrances.

Words of Unbelief

"And one of the multitude answered and said, "Master, I have brought unto thee my son, which hath a dumb spirit; and wheresoever he taketh him, he teareth him; and he foameth, and gnasheth with his teeth, and pineth away; and I spake to thy disciples that they should cast him out; and they could not." He answereth him, and saith, "O faithless generation, how long shall I be with you? How long shall I suffer you? Bring him unto Me." And they brought him unto Him, and when He saw him, straightway the spirit tare him; and he fell to the ground, and wallowed foaming.

"And He asked his father, "How long is it ago since this came unto him?" And he said, "Of a child. And ofttimes it cast him into the fire and into the waters, to destroy him, but if thou canst do anything, have compassion on us and help us."

Jesus said unto him (the father), "If thou canst believe, all things are possible to him that believeth." And straightway the father of the child cried out and said with tears, "Lord, I believe, help thou mine unbelief." When Jesus saw that the people came running together, he rebuked the foul spirit, saying unto him, "Thou dumb and deaf spirit, I charge thee, come out of him, and enter no more into him." And the spirit cried and rent him sore, and came out of him; and he was as one dead, insomuch that many said, "He is dead." But Jesus took him by the hand, and lifted him up; and he arose."

–Mark 9:17-27

We see in this portion of Scripture what a man's word can produce. The father of the deaf and dumb boy first gave a negative confession. He said, *"If thou canst do anything, have compassion on us and help us."* These certainly were not words of faith but rather of despair and hopelessness. Despair or hoping will not move the hand of God, but faith and words of faith will.

Notice the picture here. The moment the father and his son approach Jesus, the child goes into a fit. The young lad is thrown to the ground by this powerful demon. Jesus saw the demon tearing the boy, yet He made no immediate effort to relieve the suffering of the boy, but rather turned to this despairing father only to question him. From the lips of this man came a faithless, negative phrase, *"if thou canst do anything…"* Faith does not speak this way. Only unbelief speaks with an *"If thou canst"* expression. Faith says, "I know You can and will deliver me!" When Jesus heard the faithless words of this father He answered with twelve words only, *"If thou canst believe, all things are possible to him that believeth."* These powerful words drove out the unbelief from this father and he cried out, *"Lord, I believe…"* Because of the words of faith from this man's lips, Jesus could deliver his boy. God is waiting for us to confess our faith in Him so He will be able to give us *"the desires of our heart and satisfy our mouth with good things"* (Psalms 37:4, 103:5).

Saying what God Says

Christianity is called the confession. In Hebrews 3:1 we read, *"Consider the apostle and high priest of our confession* (or profession*)..."* Confession means to "say the same" or "to speak accordingly." When we refer to Christianity as being a confession, we mean to speak according to what God says concerning us. We are to say what God says about our body, soul and spirit. Confession is saying what God says, or saying what the Word of God says.

> *"The word is nigh thee, even in thy mouth, and in thy heart; that is, the word of faith, which we preach; that if thou shalt confess with thy mouth the Lord Jesus (Jesus as Lord), and shalt believe in thine heart that God hath raised Him from the dead, thou shalt be saved. For with the heart man believeth unto righteousness; and with the mouth confession is made unto salvation."*
>
> —Romans 10:8-10

The word "saved" comes from a Greek word called "sozo." This word "sozo" means "to save, deliver, protect, heal, preserve, do well, to make whole." In Romans 10:9, the Word of God declares that if we will confess with our mouth Jesus as our Lord and Savior and believe it in our hearts, we will be saved. It can also mean that if we confess Christ as our Healer, we shall be healed. If we confess Christ with our mouth as our Protector, we shall be protected. If we confess with our mouth the Lord as our Shepherd, we will not want. Romans 10:10 states, *"confession is made unto salvation."* The word salvation is taken from a Greek word called "soteria." The meaning of this word is "to rescue, deliver, save, safety and health." Salvation doesn't come until we confess Christ as our Savior. Neither does healing come until we confess Christ as our Healer.

Our confession of Christ as our Savior brings to pass the new birth and the forgiveness of sins. We can't be "born again" until we have confessed with our mouth that Christ Jesus is Lord and Savior. We also must confess Christ as our Healer before we can be healed. Even though our body may be in pain we must confess, "*by His stripes*" I am healed, and "*I am the Lord that healeth thee*" (1 Peter 2:24; Exodus 15:26). This will always produce healing, salvation, etc., if we believe what we are confessing.

All of God's blessings and promises must be applied in the same way. If we are weak in strength, we are to confess Christ as our strength before we will receive His strength in our body. "*The Lord is my strength*" (Psalms 28:7). When it appears that we are going to be defeated in some physical or spiritual battle, that is the time to say what God says about our condition. Romans 8:37, "*Nay, in all these things we are more than conquerors through Him that loved us,*" and, "*If God be for us, who can be against us*" (Romans 8:31). When we believe and confess what God says about our battles, then we will become a conqueror in our battles. When we are lacking financially and it looks like our family may go hungry or our business may go bankrupt, then is the time to confess what God says about our financial condition. "*My God shall supply all your need according to His riches in glory*" (Philippians 4:19). When we believe and confess these words, there are not enough devils in hell to stop God from supplying our needs. God's Word will not fail. "*For I am the Lord: I will speak, and the word that I shall speak shall come to pass*" (Ezekiel 12:25).

Confessing the Wrong Thing

Too many Christians confess their weaknesses and their failures. We talk about our lack of this and that; we talk about our aches and pains. We talk about our sickness and our symptoms. We talk about how hard the devil is making it for us. We talk of not having enough money. We talk of how we are in want. We talk about how hard it is to serve God. We use our mouth to confess what we feel, think and believe. We often take no regard to what God says about our condition. But if we would stop and think about what we are about to say, we would be shocked to discover our confession is often contrary to God's Word.

Who Are We?

Many Christians believe they are like a worm of the dust. They lack confidence before God and feel unworthy. But God declares that you and I are the *"sons of God,"* and *"joint heirs with Christ"* (1 John 3:2; Romans 8:17). Many believe that it is God's will for them to be in poverty and sickness. But of course this is not true. God wants you to prosper and be in health. Don't say that the Lord is making you poor or sick. You are not poor for God's glory and neither are you sick for God's glory. The devil is the one that wants you to go hungry and live in want. The devil is the one that brings diseases upon you. God declares His highest desire for you, his sons and daughters, is that you prosper and be in health. Think of it, God wants you to prosper financially. God wants you to be in health.

> *"Beloved I wish above all things that thou mayest prosper and be in health, even as thy soul prospereth."*
>
> −3 John 1:3

God wants you in health. Believe it and confess it! "It shall come to pass." We cannot rise any higher than our confession. If we believe and confess things that are contrary to God's Word, we can expect only contrary results. Negative confessions bring negative results.

The Sin of Unbelief

Fear always causes unbelief, and unbelief always breeds more fear. When we verbalize our unbelief we will live in a state of fear; fearing that God won't heal my body; fearing that God won't save my soul; fearing that God won't supply my needs; fearing that God won't protect me. This is unbelief, and God calls it sin. *"Whatsoever is not of faith is sin"* (Romans 14:23). You will never live in a realm higher than your confession. Remember the Bible says, *"As a man thinketh in his heart, so is he,"* and *"out of the abundance of the heart the mouth speaketh"* (Proverbs 23:7; Matthew 12:34).

Yes Lord, Let it Be So

As Jesus passed two blind men, they cried out to Him: *"Thou Son of David, have mercy on us"* (Matthew 9:23-30). Jesus knew what they wanted because he could see their condition—they were blind. But He asked them anyway, *"Believe ye that I am able to do this?"* Their answer was, *"Yea Lord."* It was this faith confession that set them free from this blind spirit. A faith confession can set you free from any bondage Satan has you in. I doubt if the blind men would have been healed if they had said, "I hope so," or "I am trying to believe." Words of unbelief will only strengthen the chains of Satan about you. But powerful words of faith will break them asunder and set you free!

What do you Believe the Most?

I have often been asked what we should do if, after prayer, the pain is still there? People ask, "If the pain doesn't leave, does that mean that I didn't get healed?" What do you believe the most—the Word of God or the pain? In what are you having faith—the Word or the symptoms? The Bible declares that *"heaven and earth shall pass away"* but the Word of God will not fail. I would rather believe God's Word than to believe my aches and pains. The Word of God will drive out all pain, all symptoms, all sickness, all disease and all the rest of Satan's torments. But in order for you to receive that deliverance you must believe and confess the Word of God right in the face of your pain and your symptoms.

All fear, unbelief, pain, sickness, want and Satan himself will flee when you and I confess the Word. The Bible says, *"Resist the devil, and he will flee from you"* (James 4:7). How do we resist the devil? Do we resist him through medicines? Do we resist him through having an operation? How did Jesus resist the devil?

The fourth chapter of Luke tells us. Satan came to Jesus after

Christ has finished a forty-day fast. Satan suggested He turn stones to bread, if He was the Son of God. Jesus resisted Satan with the Word of God. Luke 4:4, *"And Jesus answered him, saying 'It is written, that man shall not live by bread alone, but by every Word of God.'"* Satan then told Jesus to worship him and he would give Him all the power and glory of the Kingdoms of the world. Jesus resisted the devil through the Word of God. *"It is written, thou shalt worship the Lord thy God, and Him only shalt thou serve."*

Just think of it, even Jesus Christ, God's own Son, used the Word of God in resisting the devil. If Jesus resisted the devil by God's Word so should you and I. God's Word on your lips of faith are just as strong as if Jesus was speaking them Himself. The Word on the lips of Jesus caused Satan to flee. God's Word on your lips of faith will do the same for you.

The testimonies of numbers of people who were healed, some recorded in this book, were from the mouths of people who were continually confessing the Word. When they received prayer, they spoke the Word. When they went home, they confessed the Scriptures. When symptoms tried to return, they declared the promises of God! And when others asked how they were doing, their words were always filled with thanksgiving and praise to God for their healing.

Confess the Word. Use the Word of God in your battles. Use the Word of God in your prayer life. Use the Word of God against the devil. Turn your defeats into victories. Turn your failure into success. Turn your sickness into health. Turn your poverty into prosperity. Turn your fears into faith. Destroy your unbelief by believing and confessing the Word of God.

Summary

1. **Out of the abundance of the heart, the mouth speaks.**
2. **We are not to let unbelieving words out of our mouth.**
3. **We are to say what God says.**
4. **We are the children of God and the healed of the Lord.**
5. **Sickness and symptoms will disappear as I confess the Word of God.**

Faith Confessions

*   I believe the Lord is My Healer, He is my great Physician.
*   I believe that Jesus took my sicknesses in His body on the cross.
*   He took my infirmities and bore my sicknesses (and carried my pains).
*   If Jesus took it, I don't have to.
*   I believe that the Lord will take sickness away from me and He will not permit any of the diseases He brings on the wicked.
*   I am a child of God and my inheritance is healing. It is the children's bread.
*   It is God's will to heal me. He is willing and able to heal me completely.
*   I thank God that my healing was paid for 2000 years ago and I receive it now by faith.
*   I have faith to be healed and I receive it now.
*   I will not listen to symptoms in my body, but I will listen to the Word of God.
*   I fight the good fight of faith.
*   I resist the devil and his sickness. He must flee.
*   I trust in Jesus Christ who went about doing good and healing all who were oppressed of the devil.
*   Jesus Christ is the same yesterday, today and forever!
*   He is my Healer and I am healed!

CHAPTER VII

The Power of a Renewed Mind

"Jesus Christ, the same yesterday, today and forever."
—Hebrews 13:8

People often wonder if it is the evangelist or the believer who makes the healing happen. Well, of course, it is neither. Jesus makes the healing happen. But who is most responsible for the faith to believe for that miracle? Sometimes I had great faith and it seemed that it was my faith that released the healing power of God in people's lives as we prayed for them at our altars. Other times, and probably more frequently, it was the faith of the person coming for healing which brought about the healing work in their body. It is so important for the seeker to have faith that Jesus can heal them. When people had a mind that was set on healing and a confession of faith in their mouth, miracles happened.

It is a pathetic thing, yet often true, that more negative talk is found in the church than outside the church. And yet we call ourselves believers! No wonder Paul speaks about the *"renewing of your mind"* because he realized the power of right thinking! The right mindset is of vast importance to the Christian in obtaining the promises of God! Unless we have a positive attitude toward God's Word, healing will never become a reality. How important then is a positive attitude. That kind of attitude has great reward. That kind of a renewed mind is God's will for the believer. It does not know defeat!

> *"And be not conformed to this world: but be ye transformed*
> *by the renewing of your mind, that ye may prove what is that*
> *good, and acceptable, and perfect, will of God."*
>
> —Romans 12:2

> *"And be renewed in the spirit of your mind"*
>
> —Ephesians 4:22-24

If, right now, you will take a positive attitude toward God's prom-ise to heal, it will move God to begin working on your behalf. The moment we get positive and act on our faith, it turns God in our direction!

To those of us who have been in habitual negative thinking for a long time, it means nurturing an entirely new and positive stand. Refuse to listen to Satan's negative suggestions. Fill your mind with God's thoughts! Talk God's language! Delighting yourself in the Lord and becoming a positive thinking person will give you your heart's desire. If you desire healing, get positive!

Rid yourself of every negative, faith-destroying thought. Imme-diately fill that emptied capacity with creative and positive thoughts, God's thoughts, and God's promises! If Satan has whispered nega-tive things in our mind for so long, the only way to combat him is to permeate our mind with good positive, faith-filled thinking, until there is no more room for faith-destroying notions.

Be on Guard

Be on constant guard over Satan injecting negative thoughts into your mind! Safeguard your words by letting only positive, life-giving words come out of your mouth, blessing others. The Scripture tells us, *"we have the mind of Christ!"* If we have the mind or thoughts of Christ, then we are going to use words and talk like Christ. Paul knew the power of the mind.

> *"Casting down imaginations, and every high thing that ex-*
> *alteth itself against the knowledge of God, and bringing into*

captivity every thought to the obedience of Christ."

–2 Corinthians 10:5

We are not to let our thoughts run in a negative channel, but corral those thoughts that run rampant, causing them to become subordinate to the Holy Spirit! Do not say, as many say, that we cannot control our mind or our words.

> *"He that hath no rule over his own spirit is like a city that is broken down, and without walls"*
>
> –Proverbs 25:28

> *"Thou are snared with the words of thy mouth, thou are taken with the words of thy mouth"*
>
> –Proverbs 6:2

> *"Pleasant words are as a honeycomb, sweet to the soul, and health to the bones."*
>
> –Proverbs 16:24

Meditate upon these three Scriptures. Realize the difference the positive position or the negative position plays in these Scriptures. Words have the power to literally bring health to our bodies.

What is Your Will?

It is impossible for Satan to rob you of your rightful, promised healing, unless you let him! Because God gave man a free will, man has the power of choice. God intended man to use that God-given free will in the right way! It was to be a blessing to mankind, not to be wrongly used, and thus become a hindrance.

The final decision of our healing rests in our own hands. God has already done His part. Now it is up to us to do our part, and our part is the easy part. This is where our will enters—in the acceptance of God's promise. Unless we will to accept, healing never will be ours. It is by our own decisive will that we are kept in captivity or loosed from our sicknesses.

This will, although God-given, is often a great hindrance in our lives, because we can use our will wrongly. One writer declared,

> *"Although great emphasis has been stressed upon the wonder of Jesus walking upon the waters, and His feeding of the multitudes, the quieting of the storm upon His spoken word, yet in the eyes of heaven those miracles were of the smallest importance! Nature was the servant of Jesus, and over it and the material world, He had absolute control. Jesus' acts were not premeditated where those of nature were concerned. But His real miracle work is in the hearts of men! There He is limited by the Father's own gift to mankind, the gift of free will. He cannot command man as He commands the waves!"*

Think of it, friend. You can block God's miracle power in your own life through wrong use of your will! Things of a negative nature are the greatest blockage that Satan can suggest. Keep the channel clear and open with a strong, wholesome, positive attitude, and by so doing, declare your desired healing! Will to do it!

God has done His Part—Now it's up to Us

God could force His healing upon you, but since He has given you a will, you alone are the one to decide and act on this promise of healing. Were God to bypass our own will, and force His blessing upon us, what fellowship then would there be between God and His children? God made man for fellowship—that is why it was necessary for God to include a free-will in man's make-up. Otherwise His children would be as "puppets" pulled into action at God's command! There would be no voluntary fellowship, no response to the Father's love, were that the case.

I watched hundreds and perhaps thousands of people listen to the Word of God and walk out of our meetings filled with hope and with faith. Later we received written testimonies of how God healed so many of those people, even after they left our meetings. You can be like one of those people of faith. You can read this book, lay it down, go to sleep and wake up healed. You can begin walking in faith and confessing the Word of God and all of a sudden find yourself healed and healthy.

Our healing then is virtually in our hands, since God has already provided healing through what Jesus did for us on the cross. You can will to be healed, or you can will to remain sick, but God wills you to be well!

> *"Beloved, I wish above all things that thou mayest prosper and be in health, even as thy soul prospereth"*
>
> −3 John 2

Get positive about God's promises. If you want a healing, get positive! If you want happiness, get positive! If you want to be a blessing, get positive! Discard that negative outlook. Cultivate a positive, faith-filled attitude and then watch the answer to your prayers become a reality! Think, talk, and act in God's terms and you will get Bible results!

Summary

1. **Fill our minds with positive, faith-filled thoughts.**
2. **Guard ourselves against negative thoughts of unbelief.**
3. **Set your will to receive your healing.**
4. **God has done His part for our healing, now let's do our part.**

> *"Father we pray for all who read this book, that a powerful spirit of faith will come upon them and they will rise up out of any negative or unbelieving spirit and begin to possess what is rightfully theirs.*
>
> *"We pray for signs, wonders and healings to follow the Word as they have received it through this text. We pray a blessing, the blessing of Abraham, and a blessing of health and prosperity upon all who read, and all who believe.*
>
> *"In Jesus' Name, Amen!"*

CHAPTER VIII

Modern Day Miracles and Healings

Crooked Spine Healed

Dear Brother Iverson,

I want to tell you about my healing that it may inspire someone else to have faith. I have suffered this past twelve years with a weak back, and when I went to the hospital I had it x-rayed. They told me I had a crooked spine, but that they were sorry they could do nothing for me. I would have to wear a support and even this did not give me any relief. Then I saw in our local paper about your Healing Campaign in our city. So I attended the service on 30th July and I went up into the healing line. I believed that God would heal me and as soon as you placed your hands on me and prayed the pain left immediately. Thank God He did answer prayer. At 2:30 a.m. the next morning I awakened out of my sleep and first my head got very dizzy and then I felt the bone in my spine going into place and since then I have never had any trouble with my back, Praise God. I have proved that every day with Jesus is sweeter than the day before.

Hannah Moore,
Tyrone, North Ireland
(This testimony was confirmed months after the healing took place.)

Healed of Paralysis

Dear Brother Iverson,

I would like to tell you how I have been healed after suffering for three years with paralysis. I was twenty-one weeks in the hospital and could not get in or out of bed. I cried for over six weeks thinking I would never be able to walk again.

I read in the daily paper that Brother K.R. Iverson was coming to our town. I was taken to him and joined in the prayer line. He said if we gave ourselves up to Jesus we would be healed. He prayed to God with me that I would be healed. That night I was restored back to health, thanks be to God.

James Cook
Dungannon, North Ireland
(This man was strong and healthy six months after his deliverance.)

Healed of Epilepsy Attacks

I want to give all the praise to the Lord for healing me of epilepsy two years ago. I had doctored for thirteen years, and yet the spells were getting closer together and more violent. The doctor told me there was nothing that could be done, although I was doctoring constantly. In December, 1951, I had two violent spells within one hour. I heard the message of deliverance, and was healed instantly. All the symptoms left immediately and have never returned! I have taken no medicine since and I am much stronger and healthier than I ever had been in all of my life. I give God all the glory and praise.

Mrs. Bonnie Bartrug,
Portland, OR USA

Destroyed Eye Healed by God's Power

Dear Brother Iverson,

I want to tell you how the Lord healed my son Stanley in the last night of your campaign in Armagh City. Going through a hedge, a thorn slapped back and completely destroyed the sight of his right eye. We believed God would heal him and brought him in the healing line for prayer. After you prayed for him, he could see your hand. It is now two weeks later and God has completely delivered him. Praise God, He still heals today, and He is still on the throne. God bless you, Brother Iverson for your prayers, and may God continue to use you to bring Bible deliverance to His people.

Mr. Bill Gray
Lurgan, N. Ireland

God Performs Operation on Stomach

Seven months ago I was booked for an operation for internal trouble. I came to Brother Iverson's mission in Dungannon and was saved and healed in one night. On my way in to be prayed for I destroyed my hospital card, and two days later I rang the hospital and told them to tell the surgeon that the operation would not be necessary. At this time I had no results of my healing, but I had "faith." There was actually three things to be done in that operation, and praise God I had three healings. When I was prayed for the power of God went right through my body and I know God had touched me and healed my body. You know it's wonderful what prayer can do.

Mrs. R. Cranston,
Coalisland, North Ireland

Ear Deaf for Fifteen Years is now Hearing

My one ear had been completely deaf for fifteen years. While working for a logging company I was hit on the head by a large swinging crane. Doctors said there was nothing that could be done to restore the hearing in that ear. One doctor even said that in time the hearing would be impaired in the other ear, and I would go completely deaf.

I was a Christian and knew God was able to heal…but certainly never knew His will concerning healing. I just took it for granted I'd never hear again in that one ear, and in time would lose my hearing altogether. The Iversons were holding a Healing Campaign in the Armory at Lebanon, Oregon, and after attending a meeting there for the first time I knew it was God's will to heal! I went up for prayer and God restored the hearing in that deaf ear.

Mr. Hugh Bailey
Sweet Home, OR USA

I wish to confirm Hugh Bailey's testimony. I have known Hugh for around ten years, and knew he was totally deaf in one ear, due to an accident prior to the time I first met him.

I heard about the Iverson healing Campaign in Lebanon, and attended three or four meetings, and then brought them the Bailey's with me. In fact, I brought them the night Hugh received his hearing.

I do testify to the fact of Hugh Bailey being totally deaf in one ear, and after prayer was delivered.

Mr. W.E. Bush
Sweet Home, OR USA

Woman Healed of Diabetes

Dear Brother Iverson,

One night I attended your Bible Deliverance Campaign in the City of Armagh. I was in need of healing of diabetes. That night when you prayed the Lord healed me and when I went home I threw the needles in the fires and haven't used them since. Praise the Lord for my healing.

(This testimony was confirmed six months after she was healed.)

Delivered from a bad Stomach
after Ten Years of Suffering

Dear Brother Iverson,

I want to praise the Lord for what He has done for me during the meeting conducted by you and Brother Davidson in Armagh, during August of last year. I was suffering with my stomach for about ten years which gave me a lot of pain. I had attended doctor after doctor. I had x-rays scores of times, but they were unable to help me in any way. I went to an Herbalist who told me I had cancer. After treating me for six months I was no better. Then I heard of your meetings. I attended for a few nights and saw the wonderful healings taking place. The following night when you called the prayer line I went out for prayer, believing God that when you would lay your hands on me I would be healed. When you prayed for me I felt the power of God go right through me and the Lord healed me. I have now gained fourteen pounds. Praise His wonderful name. May He continue to bless and you for His glory.

E. A. Busby
Dungannon, North Ireland

Healed of Back Trouble

Dear Friends,

I would just like to say how grateful I am to the Lord for all His blessing. I attended your deliverance campaign in the City of Armagh where I once again felt the healing power of God. I received strength to my back that had been weak from birth, and is now perfectly straight. I give Him all the praise.

W.H. Lloyd
Killyman, North Ireland
(This testimony was confirmed months after the healing took place.)

Arthritis of the Spine Healed by God

Dear Brother in the Lord,

Just a few lines of testimony concerning the way I was healed. I was laid aside for twelve years with arthritis of the spine and the disc was gone to left of spine. I had been examined by doctors and specialists, and my own specialist decided on sending me to the Hospital, and when there I was x-rayed, and the disc to left of spine was gone. He was going to perform an operation, and when he saw he could not do so he said all he could do for me was to put a special spinal brace on me, enabling me to walk around. I wore the brace for five years. Then Brother Iverson came to Dungannon, and I heard about him, and decided that I would go and hear him. My second night I went in the faith and strength of the Lord and prayed earnestly that the Lord would heal me. Praise God I stood up and the Lord touched my body and healed me. I could feel the heat rising up where I was standing. With the result I came home, cast away my cane and took my spinal brace off. That was the fifth of September, and praise God from the depth of my heart I am healed and rejoicing in the Lord ever since. Every day my faith grows stronger in the Lord. I trust this testimony will be a blessing to some soul.

Robert J. Williamson
Tyrone, North Ireland
(This man was healed the 5th of September, 1954. He gave us his testimony March, 1955, and his healing was complete.)

Deaf Ear Opened

Beloved Brother in Christ,

My simple testimony to the healing power of Jesus for my ear in your Armagh meetings. You will remember saying there was someone present deaf in one ear, and that if they came forward God would heal them. I claimed healing according to His word, so when you laid on your hands on my ears and spoke to me on the deaf side I could find my own voice sounding through my deaf ear, and could hear the words you spoke. I was told some time ago by a professor that were was nothing could be done, but I have learned to believe God, who as said, "All things are possible." Praise God for His truth which sets us free.

Mrs. M. Turkington,
Armagh, North Ireland
(This testimony was confirmed six months after God had opened her deaf ear. She has been attending church and hearing every word the preacher says.)

No Need for Cane, Healed of Arthritis

Dear Brother,

I have had arthritis pains for the past six years. I was invited to go to your Bible Deliverance Campaign. I put my faith in God and He delivered me from these pains, and now I am able to walk without the aid of a stick.

Mrs. E. M. Shaw,
Dungannon, North Ireland
(This testimony was confirmed six months later.)

Healed of Eye Trouble

"By His stripes I am healed." Three years ago I was having a trying time with my eyes. It was a nerve strain that worked a double hardship since my work involves much driving. I heard the message of deliverance, so I acted my faith in God's word, and removed my glasses. They were bifocals and I had worn them for years. From that very hour my eyes stated to mend. Today I can read longer without eye strain than I ever could with the best glasses I ever wore. I praise Him for victory in Jesus.

Rev. W.L. Hanson
Portland, Oregon USA

Little Girl Burned with boiling tea
Healed by the Prayer of Faith

Dear Brother Iverson,

My little girl got badly burned with a tea pot of boiling tea, across her lungs, her arm, the back of her head, and her hand. There was a large mass of large water blisters and her arm became very bad. The doctor said that septic was setting in and she would have to go to the hospital. I believed the Lord to whom nothing is too hard could heal her. I brought her to the healing service in the Town Hall, and had her prayed for. Praise the Lord He answered our prayers, for that very night the blisters that were to be cut off all went flat and all the swelling went down. When I brought her to the doctor to get the burns on her back and arm dressed, all signs of septic had gone and she didn't have to go to the hospital. Praise the Lord.

Mrs. E. Gibson
Portadown, North Ireland

Delivered from the Effects of Rheumatic Fever

I am so thankful to God for delivering my body as well as my soul. I was a young girl still in my teens when I had an attack of Rheumatic fever, and for eighteen months I was unable to work. Thank God He restored me, but since that time some twelve years ago I had almost continual pain and weakness in my left arm and wrist, which at times was very hard to bear. Thanks be to God when I realized that the Lord who saved my soul could also heal my body, I went up in the prayer line. When I was prayed for, oh, what a change came into my wrist and arm. What a joy and thrill in my soul. Truly I can say the Lord is wonderful.

Mrs. E. Francis White
Dungannon, North Ireland
(This testimony was confirmed a month after the healing, and our sister's wrist and arm are free from all pain.)

Healed by a Prayer Cloth

Dear Evangelist and Mrs. Iverson,

I received your letter and I wore the stripe (cloth) for seven days in the name of the Lord. The pain below my heart which I had for over four years went away on the third day. I have never felt it since, thank God. I thank the Lord night and morning for what He has done for me. I read a chapter of the Bible every night when I come home from work. I am very thankful to you and the Mrs. For praying for me. I have given your name and address to five different people who are ailing, and they will write to you. If there is anything that I can do to help your good work I will always be willing to do it.

Mrs. F.E. Hobson
Hamiltonsbawn, North Ireland

Healed in our Mass Prayer Services

Dear Mr. Iverson,

I praise God He not only saves and keeps us, but He is able to heal our bodies too if we have faith to believe on His word. I have suffered from hoarseness in my throat for a number of years. It would give me trouble when I would sing. On Sunday night as you made the appeal to those who were ill in any way to stand to their feet and have faith to believe God will heal them. I stood to my feet and thank God He has healed me and delivered me of my complaint. To God be the glory, great things He has done. May God richly bless you.

Mrs. Moore
Dungannon, North Ireland
(This testimony confirmed six months after she was healed. She now can sing without any hoarseness.)

Christ the Same

Filled with a strange new hope they came,
The blind, the leper, the sick, the lame.
Frail of body, spent of soul,
As many touched Him were made perfectly whole.
The Christ we follow is still the same,
With blessings that all who will may claim.
How often we miss love's healing touch,
By thinking, "We must not ask too much."
By Edith Reid

Martin Luther

Feelings come and feelings go
And feelings are deceiving,
My warrant is the Word of God,
Nought else is worth believing.

Though all my heart should feel condemned
For want of some sure token,
There is One greater than my heart,
Whose Word cannot be broken.

I'll trust in His unchanging Word,
Til soul and body sever.
For though all things shall pass away,
His Word will stand forever!

CHAPTER IX

Interview on Healing

Pastor Wendell Smith interviewed Pastor K.R. "Dick" Iverson on his healing ministry.

Pastors Wendell & Gini Smith, and Rev. Dick & Edie Iverson

The beginning of your ministry was marked by the healing power of God. What was that like in your early days and when was that?

Dick Iverson: 1948 was the first encounter I had with the supernatural, as far as anything earth-shaking. Because I was raised Pentecostal we prayed for the sick all the time and we were more like the prophets of Baal, just screaming and yelling and hoping it would work. We thought noise was power.

But I saw William Branham for the first time when I was 18 years old. I was sitting beside my pastor, T.L. Osborn, who was six years older than I was, and William Branham prayed for deaf and dumb people who instantly began to talk and hear. The supernatural anointing on that stage of the Civic Auditorium in Portland, Oregon was just overwhelming. And that's actually when T.L. Osborn locked himself in his bedroom and said, "I'm not coming out until I hear from God, because if God can do this for William Branham, he can do it for me."

I was 18 and I didn't know how I was going to get started, but my heart was definitely motivated by what I had seen in a very tangible way—by the power of God. I wanted to be involved in that kind of ministry. So it was about a year later when my pastor T.L. Osborn, who by that time was in the healing ministry, called and wanted to know if I would come and join him as a tent boy in his tent that would seat 8,000 people. I saw that as a wonderful opportunity, and maybe a way to get into the ministry. In that day we didn't have any of the teaching we enjoy today as far as mentoring, so I was just being mentored by what I saw. And so I joined Brother Osborn when I was 19 and we traveled different places. My job was to help the sick up and down the stairs so he could pray for them. I sat under his ministry for about six months and that's where I was trained. He was very much a Word man. He didn't claim to have any gifts. Some people had vibrations in their hands and all kinds of different subjective things. But he simply said, "I don't have any gifts, I've just got the word of God. And if you will believe it with me, miracles will happen." So that is really what put me into the ministry as well because I didn't have any angelic visitations like William Branham, just, "it's the Bible and if we can get people to believe it, then things will happen."

Where did this take place?

Iverson: This started in Reading, Pennsylvania, in 1949 and like I say, I was 19 at the time. So, I traveled with Brother Osborn and when he went to Jamaica I thought this would be my chance. But you know, who's going to ask a 19 year old to come hold a crusade or revival? And of course I hadn't even spoken by that time. I just was a tent boy. But I was storing up the Word of God in me and I believed it. I went to Jamaica hoping that maybe somewhere in the bush, at least, I could get started preaching and praying for the sick. So that's really what happened.

A door opened in what was then called the Barbican Baptist Church on the edge of Kingston. The local pastor was unable to fill his pulpit and they said I could go down there and preach and hold a healing revival. T.L. was in the big Stadium Crusade and this little church was at the edge of Kingston. That's where I started preaching. I nailed up a piece of cardboard that said "K. R. Iverson, Divine Healing Campaign starts on Sunday night" and then I realized, "Wow, I'm the preacher!" I spent the rest of that week waiting for Sunday to come, fasting and praying because it was real simple. Either I could preach or I couldn't. Either God would heal or He wouldn't. And if He didn't then I was going to go home and marry my little blonde girlfriend I had been dating for three years. So that's how I started in that little Baptist Church in Kingston, Jamaica.

How long were you there before you got married and then went to Northern Ireland?

Iverson: I stayed January, February, March and April and came home in May of that year to get married to Edie that summer, which I did. Then we went back, in 1951, to Jamaica. It was the only door I had open so I went back to Jamaica and started preaching in the bush near Kingston and Montego Bay and in different places throughout Jamaica and we had a great time. These were not the tens of thousands but there were hundreds of people and I prayed for the sick and they got healed.

I remember praying for one blind lady who thought I was in love with her. She got healed and then thought since I healed her that I loved her. She wanted Edie to go home because I loved her and I healed her eye. She stood outside of our house and that's when they said, "Why are you there?" And she said, "Well he loves me. He healed my eye." "No, he didn't heal your eye. Jesus did that." But that's how it all started and then we returned to Portland.

And then Northern Ireland came into focus which was supernatural. Every time in my life when I have fasted and prayed seriously, God has spoken to me. This was fasting for not just a week, and not a two- or three-day fast (I've done a lot of those). But I went on a three-week fast by myself after I was married because I'd been to Jamaica and now I had no other contacts. And the Lord spoke to me during these weeks of fasting by this little brook, "Within a year you'll be on foreign soil." That's all He said to me and I knew it was God. I wrote everything down during that fast. And then I actually spun a globe. I was so sure God would tell me where I would be going to go and He basically said, "Go back and take care of your Father's sheep." Well I didn't want to hear that, but He also said "Within a year you'll be on foreign soil." So at the end of that time I spun this globe, just playing with it, and my finger stopped the spinning and there right above my fingernail was Ireland.

I didn't know if the Irish even spoke English! I'd heard of Gaelic, but I never thought anything more about it. That was in that summer but the Lord had said "within a year you'll be on foreign soil." About a month before that year was up, I received a letter from the pastor in Redding, Pennsylvania where I had started with Osborn and he said "I just got back from Ireland." When this letter came, the Holy Spirit just jumped in me and confirmed, "That's where you're going to go." And then I remembered the spinning globe almost 10 or 11 months before. So I wrote to the pastor and he gave me a list of names of people to contact in Ireland—"Pastor so-and-so, and pastor so-and-so" and the last name was "Willy Davidson. He delivers bread at the bread route, be sure and contact him." So I started writing letters to various pastors telling them I wanted to come and hold healing meetings. But I got through five letters and threw them all away, until I started a letter to Willy Davidson and said, "Dear Willy, I'd like to come and start a revival a week from Sunday if that's okay with you." No one teaches this in a class, you know.

I invited myself and then I realized I wouldn't even have time to get a letter back to know whether or not he would want me to come. In that day with no e-mail, we're talking 1954, I was 24 and out on the water of faith. It was quite a miracle. I just got on an airplane and flew to Northern Ireland. When I arrived in Northern Ireland, Willy Davidson had already rented a theatre, advertised my coming and was waiting for my arrival. I remember knocking on his door, having never met him, and never having even heard if he wanted me to come or not. And then this heavy-set Irishman opened the door and I wasn't sure if he would hit me, hug me or just shut the door. But he said "Oh praise God," grabbed me, lifted me off the ground and said, "I was hoping you would come because I'm not a preacher!" And that's how we started in Northern Ireland.

What year was that?

Iverson: 1954.

So you went by yourself before your wife Edie joined you?

Iverson: I went by myself and was there for about four months and God moved everywhere I went. We had a good amount of people attending the meetings with many supernatural miracles and healings. It was very unorthodox because I didn't work with any churches, which I felt bad about but the Lord helped us.

Remember in the Book of Acts where Philip went down and turned Samaria upside down with signs, wonders and many devils being cast out? I was like a Philip. But remember he later called Peter and John who came and established the church, laid hands on them and they were filled the Holy Spirit. I was like a Philip but I didn't have a Peter and John to come and establish a church and that's why I'm such a church man today because I believe I lost that harvest.

In all the places that for years were being bombed by the IRA, we held revivals and we could have had strong churches in all those places. But I didn't understand concepts about the church. I just had a healing ministry and that was it. I needed a Peter and John.

Did you feel similarly, like your mentor T. L. Osborn did, that you were just preaching the Word or did you feel like you had a gift of healing?

Iverson: No. I'm not very subjective. I'm not a prophet. I prophesy but I'm not a prophet. I've never seen any angel or had any audible voices, just inner heartfelt direction. So Brother Osborn definitely worked with churches and always has. But I didn't in those days. No church wanted me at first so I would just go in and find the biggest auditorium available—a City Hall, Town Hall, then go down to the local newspaper, take out an ad, and call up a few of the Pentecostal pastors and say, "I'm in town. Would you like to cooperate?" Some did and some didn't. But it was not a church-related meeting, which I feel bad about, but I was ignorant. I had a certain understanding of what I was doing in ministry but as far as the big picture of what God was building, I didn't have it.

What were those meetings like in Northern Ireland? Describe one of those typical healing services.

Iverson: I would go into a city of maybe 20,000, rent the Town Hall, City Hall or whatever they'd call it, and go to the newspapers, and advertise. Edie was with me when we really did a better job. The first time I started with Willy Davidson, the bread man. He would travel with me and was the song leader. He would lead the worship and then he would turn the service over to me.

But when my wife started traveling with me, Edie did the worship while I held our first child Debbie behind the curtain and then she would turn it over to me and she'd take Debbie, who was about 2 ½ at the time. So that was kind of the way it would go—pretty raw evangelism.

A lot of Christians would come because it was a healing revival. I'd preach a message of faith and healing and give a salvation altar call first and then I would say that tomorrow night we'll start praying for the sick.

I was raised under T.L.'s influence and he taught firmly that faith comes by hearing. So the people needed to hear the Word of God for a few nights before I would start ministering to the sick. Then I would start praying for the sick and believing God for miracles and healings.

But as I said, I missed the church link which later I realized. I remember walking away from hundreds of young people, college-age students, standing there saying, "Now what?" "After this revival, then what do we do?" And I would just tell them, "Well go to the church of your choice. God bless you. Good bye." That's where I lost the harvest. I mean, I had young people, 20 year olds by the dozens that could have started a church easily if I just had known what I was doing. I don't even like to talk about this, but that's why we've got to connect our healing ministries with the church today if we want the fruit to last. Yes, they got healed and I got some harvest, but not really the full harvest I believe the Lord wanted.

When you held those meetings, did you typically have a prayer line for people to come by and be prayed for? Did you lay hands on people or what was the way you operated?

Iverson: I'd give out healing cards. So I had the date the card was given. I would say, "We're going to pray for those who have been here since February 22nd" (for example). So I knew they'd been in at least two or three meetings. And I would call that group forward. I never paid any attention if they got in line without a card. At that point I just prayed for everyone. But I did try to have a system like Oral Roberts. I was greatly influenced by Dr. Roberts. He had a film called, "Venture into Faith." And I used that in my second term in Ireland and would show this film about a little boy that was healed. I got the use of that film so I would show it and then I would say "tomorrow night that's the kind of meeting we're going to have." So that was how we started our meetings during my second term over there when we spent a year in Ireland.

So, the people that influenced you obviously were William Branham in the beginning, T. L. Osborn, who was your pastor, and Oral Roberts?

Iverson: Yes and I had the privilege of meeting F.F. Bosworth, Raymond T. Richie, Gordon Lindsey and others. You know Gordon Lindsey and T. L. Osborn were together for a little while. That's one thing I really appreciate, I got to meet a lot of those healing evangelists in the 50s. The "Voice of Healing" was a great ministry. I never reached that level however because most of my ministry was in Jamaica, Bahamas and then in Cuba and the British Isles.

How long did your meetings last typically in a city?

Iverson: Two weeks would be an average. Someone gave me the philosophy "Always leave town when the meetings are at its peak. Don't wait until it goes over the hill. Your reputation will follow you." When it was really bursting, we'd close it and go to the next place. That may not have been the best, but that's what we did in those days.

With two weeks of meetings in one place, how many people, typically, would find a healing in those gatherings?

Iverson: Well, that's pretty hard to tell. I tried to get as many testimonies as we could, but in the smaller towns we would probably get 500-600 in the auditorium and we would run two services. We'd start at 6:30 and then 8:00 for the second service so we would reach 1000-1200 people for two weeks, night after night in the smaller places. Then later on we got some larger buildings that would seat three, four or five thousand.

Typically how many would come through the prayer line?

Iverson: I'd pray for a couple of hours until I was worn out. We probably prayed for 100 or, more realistically, probably 50-75 a night.

These were all evening meetings? So in the daytime would you rest and pray?

Iverson: Yes, that's exactly right. I would always take all afternoon getting ready for the evening with prayer and working on my notes and messages and so on.

Did you have certain messages that you preached a lot and recycled those as you went from town to town?

Iverson: Yes, I knew the bell ringers. I always marked at the end of my notes how many got saved or came forward to give their life to Christ with that Word. Certain messages were more effective. But here's what I learned, I remember going to one place and I was scheduled to give this good "hot" message and it was just a small crowd and I thought I'd change it and save it for the bigger crowd and the Lord spoke to me and said, "Look, if you want the bigger crowd you've got to bless these and then they'll go home and tell their friends."

I had a two-week series and I'd just go through them, basically on faith, confession of faith, healing, miracles. You know, they were filled with stories of Jesus' healings—the man at the pool of Bethesda, some things like that. I had about 21 messages and then only used about 14 of them. But I had no formal training, no Bible School, so I was scratching to come up with that many.

Did you glean from some of the other preachers you had heard?

Iverson: Yes. I gleaned from Brother T.L. I got all of his messages. And the books that I recommend that really gave me confidence which I did not have as a teenager were Kenyon's writings. Kenyon's writings gave me a spirit of faith—"In His presence," "The Father and His Family," and, "Two Kinds of Righteousness." Kenyon's writings were a tremendous help in my faith attitude because I had lived under a lot of legalism. I was always thinking I was going to hell because I had a bad thought in my mind.

You went back to Ireland a few years ago. What did you find as far as some of the fruit of your ministry or people that remembered you?

Iverson: A few years ago I was invited by James O'Connell who was the Pastor of Belfast Metropolitan Tabernacle. He wrote and asked me if I would come on his 48th anniversary. I had heard of O'Connell for a long time. This was the largest church at that time in the British Isles, which was about 4,500 people, and he wanted me to come for a particular Sunday, for his 48th anniversary. Well, I didn't think anybody was going to fly me over to Belfast, Ireland, for one day and that's all I could give him. So I wrote to him and thanked him for the invitation but I said I could only come in on one day and would have to leave the next.

But he wrote me back and said, "You don't understand, you're the reason I'm here. When I was 19 years old I followed you all over Ireland. When you left I went and started this little church in Belfast which is now 4,500 people." And it was 4,500—a huge church. So he said, "I not only want you to come. I want your wife to come," and he paid our way. So we gave him three days: Saturday, Sunday and Monday. I had 20-30 people come up to me at that anniversary and say, "I was in your meetings 50 years ago." Of course, they were all old people, "I was saved, I was healed, my mom was healed, we heard about you...." I realized my ministry had not been a total loss and it was very rewarding to see even that one church. I was so blessed to see that I had inspired the pastor like maybe Branham had inspired me. And although James O'Connell is more of an evangelist, he has raised up a very caring church and is a beautiful pastor.

What got you back into the pastoral ministry in the States since you started out as an evangelist?

Iverson: Well, the Lord tricked me. My dad had his first heart attack when I was on my way back to the British Isles. I had a home there that they let me use as long as I wanted to use it. I was going to go into Europe and evangelize the British Isles and Europe for five more years. At least that was my plan. But my dad had a heart attack and said "I want you to take my church."

What year was this?

Iverson: This would be about 1960. But of course, I didn't want to take the church because I'd been out again in evangelism and had since gone to Cuba and had some fairly big meetings. So I felt I was on my way, I was in business and my ministry was taking off. So literally on my way to the British Isles, dad suffered a heart attack and told me, "Son, I want you to take this church (in Portland, Oregon)." But I didn't want the church. Why should I preach to 100 people when the masses were waiting for me (or so I thought)? The doctors said that if I didn't get dad out of there he's going to have another heart attack and it's going to kill him. Of course, I was concerned about my dad. If I left the country and didn't take it and he were to die, I would have that on my conscience. So I said, "Okay Dad, I'll take the church." And yet I said to myself, "As soon as Dad's taillights are leaving the city of Portland, I'm going to turn this church over to the first preacher that walks through the doors."

That was my game plan, but God had another plan. He seemed to only let the con-men, the crooked preachers, come through my doors. Well, I had too much integrity to walk away from 100 people and turn them over to some wolf that would exploit them. So for almost five years I got beat up by God. I was exhausted because I tried all the church growth methods of my day—competition between the red and the blue teams, pony rides, bicycle give-a-ways for those who brought the most people. But that little church just would not move or grow.

Prophet Ernest Gentile came by and I was still in anguish. By this time I had witnessed a flow of the presence of God that was very meaningful, in Brother Reg Layzell's church (in Vancouver, Canada) and Brother David Schoch's church (in Long Beach, California) but I didn't know how to get that anointing into our house. I had brought in everybody to minister in our church—even some famous people, as far as their names were concerned, so I decided I'd bring in a prophet. At the end of his series of meeting, which was only just a few nights, Ernest Gentile said, "Pastor I have a word for you." I thought I knew what the word was. It was, "Let him go!" I could have prophesied it over myself.

But he boldly declared, "The evil that is in your heart is born of your own frustration. The problem is not the people. The problem is in you." He said this in front of our 100 people. But oddly enough, I felt good about the word. Because I knew there was some kind of problem and I was sure it was our bad batch of sheep. But he located the problem. The problem was in me!

And then a few weeks later I realized I didn't love my city and I didn't love the city of God. And if you don't love the city of man and the city of God there'll be no prophetic anointing. Boy I repented when I realized what the evil was. I went to the people and asked for forgiveness and made a commitment.

We were called "Deliverance Temple" at that time and I was still banging away at that message, but I had nothing else to say. That's a great message, as you know. But you can't build a church on an emphasis. To have that as a main part of the mentality of the church is limiting. A pastor has to teach family and missions and evangelism and the prophetic and worship and prayer and all the rest of the truths that are so helpful in building a healthy church. So I apologized to the people and said I will stay here until I die if that's what God wants. "I ask you to forgive me for not loving you." When I did that, the heavens opened and the results have been astonishing.

The presence of God came down on us and for the first time we started to grow. I fell in love with the people, the body of Christ, the Bride of Jesus and I fell in love with Portland. Even when I fly in now I just love my city of Portland.

It's been how many years now?

Iverson: That was 1965. And so, we changed our name in 1966 to "Bible Deliverance Temple," because I realized that I had been building deliverance as a total message and then we eventually dropped the word "deliverance." And that's where Bible Temple came from (later changed to City Bible Church). We still believe in deliverance, and we still believe in healing and the miraculous and all the good things of the Word of God.

What were some of the notable miracles of healing that you saw in all your travels?

Iverson: I can think of three or four. One really kicked off one of the biggest revivals I had in Ireland. We started in just little halls and a lady who had tumors throughout her body, many tumors, came up to me to be prayed for. So I prayed, rebuked the tumors in Jesus' name and cursed them and I didn't pay much attention to that. Well, she was scheduled to go back to Dublin and she was a woman who was written up in "Believe It Or Not" because she had 28 children and everybody knew her because she was on that program. But her body was just full of tumors. Of course I didn't know this. I just knew she had tumors and I rebuked the tumors in her body. She went down to Dublin for further help with the doctors. When they x-rayed her and she had, something like 40-50 tumors all over her body. But now they couldn't find them. They kept her there three days because they knew they had x-rays of all these tumors in her body and now none of them were there. I didn't even know any of this was going on. We probably had two or three hundred people at the time. So she came back and walked up with a little envelope in her hand and asked, "Can I give a little testimony?" Well I didn't know that she was known everywhere because of her 28 children. She pulled out two x-rays and showed them. I could see the little white spots on the x-rays and she said, "When I came here my body was full of tumors," and she held it up. "I went into Dublin to the doctors and they took x-rays and now there are no more tumors, they can't even find one," and she held up the other x-ray. That word spread like wildfire. The meeting kicked-off. We rented a big "Woods Product Building" they called it, which could seat 5000 people. We packed it out night after night after night with miracles and healing. They came from all over and I just kept praying for the sick. I was surprised at what God was doing, but it was just like there was this spiritual energy. I didn't feel any goose bumps. I was just praying for more and more sick folk.

And then another miracle took place—Margaret Wardell. This is who Barry White later married. She was a little girl at the time and she came up with a cleft palette. When I prayed for her, I didn't know this at the time, but they went home and the cleft palette closed up. It was a miracle!

I prayed for another lady who came up and was all bent over—a Mrs. Williams. She came up and I prayed for her. She had arthritis of the spine. She couldn't stand up straight. I remember very definitely praying for her. Nothing seemingly happened during the meeting. But that night she was awakened by a crack in her spine. The next night she walked up and said, "Do you remember me?" "No, I don't." "I'm the woman who had the curvature of the spine and last night it cracked in the middle of the night. It's been this way for years. Now my spine is straight."

And we had many things just like that. I would always start off like T.L. Osborn, praying for deafness. That's what Brother Osborn did so I had faith for deafness, and I'd pray for people who were deaf in one ear and they could hear the clock tick. That's in the days when clocks ticked! Then, as the meetings progressed, more were healed, we would have some notable miracles and the crowds grew.

Over the years since you came back and went into pastoral ministry for 40-50 years, you also have traveled around the world holding conferences and being involved in other churches. What other healings or signs have you seen and did that ministry kind of lap over into your pastoral and apostolic ministry?

<u>Iverson:</u> I would have to say it probably did because we get what we preach. You sow the seed for finances, you reap. You put in the seed for good homes, you get good homes. Whatever seed you put in—through preaching and teaching—you reap. And so now I'm a church man and I want to build churches. My themes are church government, worship, prayer, praise and so on. I don't mean in any way to diminish the healing message, but there's no question that if you would beat on that drum you're going to get more and more healing because faith comes by hearing and hearing by the word of God and as your faith so be it unto you.

There was an interesting part and I want to be real in this. Up until I was 31 it was a total healing message of course, but then I was tested to the very limit on the subject of healing. My wife, Edie, developed arthritis where I thought she's going to end up in a wheel chair. Diane, my second child, developed scoliosis of the spine, a 55% curve and she had to wear a Milwaukee brace that held her head up and then we lost Angela (one of our twins born later). This all happened the same year and I mean I was rocked to my heels, especially at the death of Angela.

I really learned something through this. I was kind of a hard-nosed preacher who taught, "If you're not healed, you didn't have enough faith." But you know I don't believe that at all. We live in faith and we die in faith. It really doesn't matter. What pleases God is faith! We want results and we expect results, but God loves faith, and He expects faith. When we cross over through the shadow of death, we do so as a believer, not an unbeliever. That's what Angela taught me. My testimony was, "The devil bruised my heel but I'm going to crush his head" and I've been busy doing that ever since.

So obviously the message of healing was tested in your life?

Iverson: Yes it was, but I never backed off. I remember T. L. Osborn saying this, "If I have 100 people lined up and I pray for 100 people and they all die, I'll get 100 more the next night and keep praying." You've got to set yourself based on the Word of God. You can't set yourself on results alone. You set yourself based on the Word of God. Results are in God's hand. He is the healer. I'm going to believe Him. I'm going to pray. I'm never going to change course.

I call it the power of the attitude of faith. It determines what you do about every situation. I just believe that God will supply, God will protect, God will heal, and God is the miracle worker. God is the deliverer. God is our salvation. God is our defense. He's our strong tower. He's everything. So my mindset is not just on the healing. If I die sick, I die; but I'm going to go in there believing there's healing in His stripes. I'm just not going to deviate from that position because I know it pleases God and I'd hate to walk in there, into the presence of The Lord and say, "You know, I quit believing about six months ago. I didn't think you even cared about me." I couldn't do that.

So when you go in there you've got to go in there as a man or woman of God, a person of faith, "I'm going to trust you and no matter what happens I'm not going to lose my faith." I lost it briefly at the death of our daughter Angela. I lost my faith, hope and love and those are the three motivating forces in life. That's what keeps you and me alive, is faith, hope and love. When you lose your faith and become hopeless and loveless, that's suicide material. You can never lose that no matter what happens.

What happened to bring that back, and for you to recover from that?

Iverson: Well, I was six weeks (although it seemed like six years) walking the floor. I shut my Bible, and I said to God, "I'm not going to be your spokesman. I'm out of here!" I was mad at God. That was during the same time I didn't love the church and didn't love the city. And then God spoke to me one night and said, *"Death is an enemy."* "Yes?" *"The last enemy to be destroyed is death."* "Yes?" *"We wait for the redemption of the body. The body is not redeemed. We wait for the redemption of the body."* And so He quoted to me Genesis 3:15 about the seed of the woman. He reminded me that the serpent would bruise his heel but the seed of the woman, which is Christ, would rise up and crush the serpent's head. And God spoke to me that night and said, *"Son, your heel has been bruised with the loss of Angela but if you'll keep your faith, I'll let you crush the serpent's head."* And faith came back in, and I said, "Ok, you bruised my heel devil, but I'll crush your head." And I've been stepping on him wherever I can ever since.

Amen! How would you suggest local church pastors can see more healings and miracles in their own churches today?

Iverson: I think my approach would be this. I love preaching a series of messages. I like to bang at a subject for months from every direction until that Spirit is in the church—whatever truth it is. I would tell pastors to take six months and just preach and teach on that truth over and over again. We never know when the stone breaks. It might be the last time and then a spirit of faith hits the church and miracles start happening. That's what I would recommend if a pastor feels that "we are just not getting through on the healing side of things."

Stay with it! Faith comes by hearing!

In fact, I remember Brother Osborn saying, "Hey, you don't need prayer. You need teaching." And that was his strong point. Often we don't need prayer. We need teaching. We've got to know it's the will of God. We've got to believe God's Scriptures and the Word and quote them over the things we're doing right now and *then* pray. But we've got to get the faith level into a place where we're expecting miracles and healings and the signs and wonders.

I wouldn't let church scandals or stories of revival meetings that went bad or evangelists who fell- bother me or destroy my faith. We know that God does the healing and people sincerely believe. People go to those meetings with faith and God honors their faith. Some people might say, "I don't trust signs and wonders any more." But that's the devil's trick—to get us to reject it all instead of holding to faith in the truth of God's Word.

What counsel would you give a young man or a young woman who maybe feels they're called to a healing ministry?

Iverson: Well I think they have to make healing their primary message and it is a great message. If you're going to pastor a church you can't just bang on that one message of course. It's only one string on the banjo. And in the overall economy of God, it might even be like a steak dinner, but we don't want steak morning, noon and night. We need a balanced diet. So a Pastor would have to preach everything.

But if you feel called to be an Evangelist or have a gift of healing and you feel that God has given you that ministry to pray for the sick and to believe for signs and wonders, then you should focus on that and give yourself to it. You should let people know that is your ministry and yet show that you still want to help build the church and submit to the authority of the House of God when you come to minister. But your message will definitely be in the area of signs and wonders and I would see no problem with that.

What words of faith would you share to help somebody who is reading this book, who might be seriously sick; they're really looking for a healing?

Iverson: Never give up. Never lose faith even til your final breath. You are there for one reason, to honor the Lord with your faith and keep the faith. Don't quit. Keep the Word of God in your heart, in your mouth, and in your mind.

Pray it out loud. Pray through the Scriptures. As I said, we've lost some wonderful people who died in faith. But as some have said, even on their death bed, "It's a win-win for me. If I live, I win. If I die, I win. I can't lose." That's a strong position, rather than, "God failed me and I don't think I believe the message anymore." No we still believe it. We live in faith! We die in faith! "The just shall live by faith".

And I would tell anybody seriously sick, don't quit, don't give up. There have been a lot of times where all seemed hopeless and then suddenly God turned people's captivity and life came back, health came back and people were gloriously healed.

CHAPTER X

Photos of Dick Iverson's Healing Meetings

Cars parked outside tent of T.L. Osborn, 1950.

Tent for Healing meetings of Evangelist T.L. Osborn, where Dick Iverson served as a tent boy, and was mentored in the Healing ministry.

Young Evangelist K.R. "Dick" Iverson (right) and his brother Neil begin healing meetings in Jamaica in 1950.

Evangelist Dick Iverson holding his first healing meeting at Barbrican Baptist Church outside of Kingston, Jamaica.

Dick Iverson with woman who was healed of a blind eye in Jamaica healing meetings.

Dick Iverson (left) as a young minister, with his brother Neil (center) and his father, Ivy Iverson (right).

Advertising Divine Healing campaign in Jamaica.

Capacity crowds gather in town halls across Ireland to hear Evangelist Dick Iverson.

(Inset) Musicians on platform lead worship services. Dick and Edie Iverson are seated on right.

Hands being raised for Salvation at Dick Iverson's meetings in Ireland.

Edie Iverson, healping her Evangelist husband, led worship in many of the healing services.

One of the many standing room only crowds gathered in Northern Ireland in the mid-fifties to hear Evangelist K.R. "Dick" Iverson, and received prayer for healing.

BIBLE DAYS ARE HERE

IN THE ARMAGH CITY HALL

A New Testament Deliverance Campaign will be Conducted by

Evangelist Keith Iverson, U.S.A.
and MR. W. DAVIDSON, Ballymena, Song Leader

From *SUNDAY, 25th JULY — SATURDAY, 31st JULY

Services each night at 8 o'clock

* Services on Sunday, 25th July, will be held in the Scout Hall, The Mal, at 3 p.m. and an Open Air Service Market Street, weather permitting) at 8.30 p.m. approx.   The City Hall being unavailable for that day.

The blind see, the deaf hear, the lame walk, the cancers are healed, and all manner of disease among the people

EVERYBODY INVITED

And these signs shall follow them that beleive.   Mark 16, 17 and 18.

Evangelist and Mrs. K. R. Iverson
U.S.A.
BIBLE DELIVERANCE CAMPAIGN

MONDAY, AUG. 8th, till 27th, 8.0 p.m. (except 14th & 15th)

LESLIE SCOTT—AT THE PIANO & CLAVOLINE

✳ SALVATION FOR SINNERS
✳ HEALING FOR THE SICK
✳ FAITH INSPIRING MESSAGES
✳ GOD'S WORD IN ACTION
✳ INTERDENOMINATIONAL

"*Jesus Christ, the same yesterday and to-day, and forever.*" Heb. 13-5.

WATCH FOR ANOTHER SHOWING—ORAL ROBERT'S FILM

"VENTURE INTO FAITH"

—— COUNTY WIDE ——
BIBLE DELIVERANCE CAMPAIGN

✳ NOVEMBER 6th through 20th, at the WOOD PRODUCT FACTORY ✳

Evangelist & Mrs. K. R. IVERSON (U.S.A.)

* LESLIE SCOTT at the Piano.
* BOB & JIM BORLAND, Gospel Singers.

* Seating Capacity 5,000.
* Salvation for Unsaved.
* Healing for Sick.
* Interdenominational.
* Miracle of Healing Nightly.

Newspaper advertisements of Evangelist K.R. Iverson from Irish papers, circa 1954.

To **THEM THAT BELIEVE**

a Message

to the Faithless
to the Fearful
to the Needy
to the Sick
to the Lost

By Evangelist **K.R. IVERSON**

One of Dick Iverson's first books, 1955.

Other Healing Resources

You Were Healed, by Dr. Wendell Smith
Healing the Sick, by Dr. T.L. Osborn
Rhema Cards

For more information & world class resources on Healing go to:
www.thecity.org